MY FATHER'S FACE

My Father's Face

A Portrait of the Perfect Father

James Robison

MULTNOMAH BOOKS • SISTERS, OREGON

MY FATHER'S FACE
published by Multnomah Books
a part of the Questar publishing family

© 1997 by James Robison

International Standard Book Number: 1-57673-030-1

Cover design by D^2 DesignWorks

Printed in the United States of America

Scripture quotations are from:
New American Standard Bible (NASB) © 1960, 1977 by the Lockman Foundation

The Holy Bible, New International Version (NIV) © 1973, 1984 by International Bible
Society, used by permission of Zondervan Publishing House

Scripture quotations marked (NLT) are taken from the *Holy Bible, New Living
Translation,* © 1996. Used by permission of Tyndale House Publishers, Inc.,
Wheaton, Illinois 60189. All rights reserved.

The Holy Bible, New Century Version (NCV) ©1991 by Word Publishing

The Message, © 1993 by Eugene H. Peterson, NavPress

The New King James Version (NKJV) © 1979, 1980, 1982 by Thomas Nelson, Inc.
Used by permission. All rights reserved.

The Living Bible (TLB) © 1971 by Tyndale House Publishers

The New Testament in Modern English, Revised Edition (Phillips) © 1972 by J. B. Phillips

The Good News Bible: The Bible in Today's English Version (TEV) © 1976
by the American Bible Society

For information:
QUESTAR PUBLISHERS, INC. • POST OFFICE BOX 1720 • SISTERS, OREGON 97759

Library of Congress Cataloging-in-Publication Data
Robison, James, 1943-
    My father's face/by James Robison.
        p.cm.
    ISBN 1-57673-030-1 (alk. paper)
    1. God--Fatherhood. 2. Robison, James, 1943- 3. Fatherhood--Religious Aspects-
-Christianity. 4. Fatherhood (Christian theology) 5. Father and child. I. Title.
BT153.F3R63   1997   97-6733
248.8'421--dc21   CIP

97 98 99 00 01 02 03 04 — 10 9 8 7 6 5 4 3 2 1

Dedication

To my wife, Betty,
and to our children and grandchildren—
Rhonda, Randy, Robin,
Terry, Debbie, Ken, Lora, Luke,
Lincoln, Laney, Christopher, Cody, Callie,
Abbie, Alek, and those to come—
in whose lives I truly see
The Father's face.

CONTENTS

ACKNOWLEDGMENTS

From the very bottom of my heart, I wish to express gratitude to all in whose lives I have seen undeniable revelations of the Father's heart. Having grown up without a father, and—as you will discover in reading this book—being born the product of extreme circumstances, I can well appreciate the glimpses of true love and the positive effect such manifestations have on the lives of those who experience them.

I wish to communicate this to no one more completely than to my own precious wife, Betty. Of all the people I have ever known or ever will know, she most closely identifies with the very heart of God in her love, devotion, and true understanding of me. I think among all of life's desires, the one most important to each of us is the desire to be understood. We want to be accepted not only when we have succeeded, but when we have failed as well. Betty has shown me the unwavering, boundless love of the true eternal and ultimate Father. I have also seen in each of our children the glorious characteristics of the Father we seek to exalt throughout the pages of this book.

In the following list of acknowledgments, I am simply expressing my appreciation for many of the people who have shown me both glimpses of glory and the revelation of God the Father.

First, I want to thank Reverend and Mrs. H. D. Hale. When I was an infant, they gave me a home and experienced the heart-rending tragedy of seeing me taken from them. Then later they opened their home again to me, as a teenage boy who had been horribly impacted by the harsh reality of the desertion of an alcoholic father and the wanderings of a truly caring mother. They showed me unwavering love and that a real family is greatly to be desired.

I also want to express gratitude for all the beautiful illustrations given to me by my own mother, Myra Hord Wattinger Robison (and believe it or not, some other married names could be added to this list). She showed me the capacity to forgive those who hurt you and to refuse to become bitter. I am thankful that she diligently pursued the goal of having the God in the Bible become real in her life. I gained tremendous sensitivity to spiritual issues through her influence.

I wish to say thanks to every person with whom I have had a brief encounter that gave me a glimpse of the Father and for all the supporters of our outreach.

Thanks to Billy Foote, the best man at my wedding, who in college saw me as a freshman and said, "I see something in you I don't see in others." He gave me a chance and helped launch a ministry that has reached to the ends of the earth. It was because of the confidence Billy expressed to me that I gained a much needed confidence in the Lord. Thanks also to his precious wife, Winky, who was my wife's maid of honor and has always been an inspiration.

I want to say thanks to Bill Baker, who was pastor of Eastview Baptist Church of Kilgore, Texas, for giving a teenage boy a chance to speak in his first series of public meetings. Thank you, Bill!

Also thanks to O. C. Robinson, who was pastor of Shiloh Terrace Baptist Church and wrote the greatest letter anyone could ever write about a young man who had just spoken in his church.

Thanks to W. A. Criswell, pastor of the great First Baptist Church, Dallas, who encouraged me continually and gave me an opportunity to begin speaking in his church on every available occasion from the time I was twenty-three years old. This privilege was the confirmation of the heavenly Father's approval. Dr. Criswell's words of encouragement to me were like fuel poured on a fire that already burned freely.

Thanks to John McKay, the great soloist, crusade song leader, and choir director who worked with me in over 500 city-wide crusades in which we ministered in person to over 15 million people. John always encouraged me, challenged me, and believed in me, and does to this day.

Thanks to John Morgan, pastor of Sagemont Baptist Church in Houston, Texas. We graduated from the same high school, and I am grateful to him for always being a friend through thick and thin. Through every circumstance,

he has been the purest, truest definition I have known of a friend who st.
closer than a brother.

Thanks also to Jim Rogers, my executive vice-president. He has always
done everything possible not only to help us walk with total integrity in every
ministry activity, but also to help me in any personal way he possibly can.
What a friend, what a loyal co-laborer! And thanks to his gifted wife, Jeanne
Rogers, who is blessed with the most wonderful soprano voice on the face of
this earth and a servant spirit willing to do anything, at any time, to help anyone. Bless you, Jeanne!

Thanks to Clayton Spriggs, who was given a home by the same Pastor
Hale and his wife who gave me a home. He has always been my friend, my
brother, my constant encourager, an ever-willing and able fellow servant.

I have the deepest gratitude for the example and friendship of Dr. Billy
Graham who prayed with me and for me, and who encouraged me to consider the possibility that God might wish to use me on television. Sure
enough, God did, and He has. Thank you, Billy!

My heartfelt thanks also to the following:

To Jerry Falwell, who invited me to speak at his great church at Thomas
Road in Lynchburg, Virginia, when I was very young, and told me that I had
a marvelous gift and gave me an opportunity to share what God had put in
my heart.

To Freddie Gage, who of course, from day one has always been an ener-
getic promoter of James Robison. He is the one who encouraged Dr. Falwell
to invite me to preach as a young man. It was Freddie who heard me preach
one of my first sermons and immediately encouraged me, wrote letters in my
behalf, and literally told people that if they didn't have me come immediately
they would certainly risk missing the very purpose of God. No one could
apply the holy heat like Freddie. What a guy! My friend, you have helped me
to see and understand the glory of the majestic Father that we talk about in
this book.

To Dudley Hall for helping me lift my voice out of a horrible pit and cry
out to the God from whose hand and heart help will surely come. Thanks to

or being a constant stabilizing force in my life. Thanks also to T. D. Hall, dley's brother. He and his wife, Sara, have always been the most wonderful, wonderful examples of Christian love. I continually see Jesus in their response to every event in life.

To Michael Ellison, who came into my life when I desperately needed the wisdom and insight of the Father to implement the vision He had planted in my heart. Also, to his wife, Susan, a consistent expression of His nature and my wife's faithful friend.

To all the wonderful pastors who have had a part in my life and ministry—those who have worked with me and those whom I, as a member of their churches, heard reveal the characteristics of the Father we all long to know. These include Sam Jones, Dr. Jimmy Draper, Slim Sullivan, Dr. Doug White, and many others whose ministries have had eternal effect on my own life. Also Milton and Joyce Green, who prayed for me and helped me find deliverance during one of the darkest hours of my life and who helped me to go back to God's Word, the Holy Bible, no longer for the purpose of finding sermons for others, but to find life abundant that could be expressed through me.

To Peter and Ann Pretorious, who showed me the other side of the world, the mission field where God's heart is so often focused and where our investments have such great effect. Together we have led millions to faith in our heavenly Father.

To Brad and Betsy Burns, who are so sensitive to God and so very unselfish in their willingness to share all that God has entrusted to them in order that the world might know the Father's heart.

To every board member who has served so faithfully at my side through the years. And a special thanks to Joe Simmons who has been my faithful friend, my buddy, and the one who can teach anyone how to dream big, no matter what the outlook.

To Jack Hayford, who so clearly demonstrated for me what fullness in the Spirit is really all about.

To John Hagee, who helped protect me from the negative effects of my own failures. Also to Jack Taylor and Jamie Buckingham, who lifted me up when I was down.

To Peter Lord, with whom I shared the secrets of my own struggles and who kept them in his heart privately while showing me the Father's ability to lift me above all enemies.

To Tommy Barnett, whose passion for souls is a constant inspiration to all and a true picture of God's compassionate care for the unredeemed.

To the entire staff of LIFE Outreach International for revealing to me how a family should relate and express the character of our great God and Father.

To Larry Libby for helping organize and edit my heartfelt feelings and expressions.

And to all those whose names I did not mention and should have, a group that numbers so many. How I pray they do not feel slighted, because every contribution made to my life continues to bring forth the fruit of that divine impartation. Perhaps the whole of this book could be filled with the names of those who have in some way enhanced my own life.

Last but not least, love and thanks to Pete Claytor who perhaps more than any other person showed me what it would be like to have an earthly father with whom to communicate. No one else on earth could have provided a better example for me. He has been brother and father figure, greatest of friends, and "fishin' pahdnah." He and his wife, Jody, have filled the biggest part of Betty's and my lives with the joy that comes with open, honest communication and true fellowship.

Glory and praise to the Father who reveals Himself to us and through us, if only we will come to know Him by looking into His face and discovering His heart.

James Robison at age 4
with his mother, Myra, and father, Joe Bailey
1947, Austin, Texas

Chapter One

My Father's Face

When You said, "Seek My face,"
My heart said to You, "Your face, LORD, I will seek."[1]

D A V I D

O n October 9, 1943, a baby was born in the charity ward of St. Joseph's hospital in Houston, Texas. The baby was the product of rape. An unemployed alcoholic living with his ailing father had forced himself on Myra Wattinger, a destitute forty-year-old practical nurse who had been caring for the older man.

Realizing she had conceived, Myra sought to terminate the pregnancy. Her doctor refused, telling her he "just didn't think it was right." In 1943, it seems, abortions were hard to come by. Not knowing how she could care for a child, the woman was at her wits end. Where should she turn? What should she do? Should she kill herself?

I can see her in my mind's eye as I write these words...on a spring night in Houston...sitting alone in an old rocker on the screened-in back porch of a boarding house...weeping softly, face in her hands, rocking back and forth, crying out to a God she desperately needed... *"Lord, I'm carrying this child, and I don't know what to do."*

God spoke comfort to Myra's heart. She felt strongly that He was speaking to her, telling her to have the baby, and that her child would—somehow—help bring joy into the world. Throughout her pregnancy she had been so convinced the baby was a little girl that she had already picked out the name: Joy.

After delivering the baby, however, the doctor said, "Lady, you can call this child anything you want to, but you've got a little boy."

I was that baby boy.

So now my mother had to come up with a different name. (Her little boy would likely have enough troubles and difficulties in life without bearing the name "Joy.") My mother asked God what she should name me. Then, possessing some Bible knowledge, she remembered that the three disciples closest to Jesus were Peter, James, and John. She wanted her son, the one God had told her would bring joy to so many people, to be close to Jesus.

"James," she said. "I'll name him James."

The birth certificate initially read James Wattinger, but Mother wanted to set the record straight. My father's name was Joe Robison, so my name would be James Robison. And after the question "Legitimate?" on the birth certificate, she indicated "no."

She was so alone.

My father, a lifelong drunkard, had returned to his bottle and oblivion. What was a baby to him? He seemed to have no concern whatever for his new son.

At that vulnerable moment in her life, my mother knew she couldn't take care of me. She had no money, no home, no prospects. Nothing. So while she was still in the hospital, she placed an ad in the *Houston Chronicle*. The simple four-line ad, which ran in the "personals" column, read:

WANTED

Loving Christian couple to raise
newborn boy. References required.

Katie Bell Hale, a Southern Baptist pastor's wife, saw the ad and didn't hesitate a moment. She got right up from her chair, hopped into her car, drove to the hospital, and brought me home. The Reverend H. D. Hale had gone deer hunting for the day, and when he came home, he had a little boy. (Pastor Hale did not go deer hunting again for twenty-three years. When I was twenty-three, I convinced him he ought to go again.)

THE FACE OF A STRANGER

Looking back on the first five years of my life, I have foggy memories of what it was like to live in a real home with the Hales. But at age five—out of the blue—the mother I had never known (even though I had visited with her briefly on earlier occasions) came back to claim me as her own, and to remove me permanently from the Hale's care. The Hales had tried again and again to adopt me, but, whatever her original intention might have been, my mother could never bring herself to sign the release papers. And now she was taking me back—for keeps.

So on the saddest day I can remember, my mother came to take me away from the only home I had ever known. I hid from her—under my bed. The Hales cried to the point of collapse as they watched a little five-year-old boy, who'd called them Mommy and Daddy since he was a baby, walk away down the driveway with a woman who was nothing more than a stranger to him.

My father had returned to his bottle and oblivion. He seemed to have no concern whatever for his new son.

We hitchhiked 175 miles from Houston to Austin because my mother didn't have enough money for bus tickets. (Clayton Spriggs, a teenage boy the Hales were caring for at the time due to family problems in his home, had tried to press a little money into my mother's hand before we left. She had refused his help.) All I had with me was my cardboard suitcase, which I still have today. I wouldn't let anybody carry that suitcase. Everything I owned was in it. It was like my identity. My mother told me I wouldn't let anyone else touch that suitcase; I just held onto it. Often, when I was tired, I would use it to sit on and rest. But I never let go of it. I may not have had any idea of where I was going or what was going to happen to me, but that little suitcase was *mine*.

Frightened and desperately homesick, I stood by the highway with a mother I barely knew. We finally landed in the Austin area, moving from place to place in the city over the next ten years. That was a decade full of instability, loneliness, and pain. I had no concept of "home." We moved so many times that I became confused about the meaning of the word. My mother often left me with people I didn't know, and every time she walked away from me I had no idea whether I'd ever see her again. I remember crying a great deal as a child.

I WANTED A DADDY

I wanted a home. I wanted a real family. And perhaps more than any-thing else, I wanted a daddy.

I *ached* for a father. I don't think I could begin to describe the pain I felt at not having a dad to call my own. I wanted someone to have me as his boy. I thought I'd be the best little buddy a daddy could ever have. I sometimes used to pretend I *did* have a daddy. A time or two, I even made the mistake of telling my friends at school that my father had taken me fishing, because I kept hearing them talking about what they'd done with their dads. Of course, he hadn't taken me fishing. I had, perhaps, been seated on the bank of a river, alone with my longing and dreams.

> *I ached for a father. I don't think I could begin to describe the pain I felt.*

I never realized my natural father had even seen me as a little boy until, years later, going through some of my mother's things, I came across an old photograph. The picture showed my mother, my father, and me, when I was very little. The picture puzzled me a great deal because—somehow—it seemed like I ought to remember something about it.

THE FACE IN THE PHOTO

In the old photograph, my own face is hardly more than a blur.

We're posing together in the snow. I can't be more than four years old. Behind me, my mother and father stand ramrod straight. My mother holds my hand, a tentative smile touching the corners of her mouth. My father, tall and severe, has a furrowed brow and the beginnings of a frown. His gloved hand is within an inch of my shoulder, but he isn't touching me at all. A white house stands behind us.

To my knowledge, it's the only picture ever taken of the three of us as a family.

As I probe the dim corners of my memory, I can recall the snow. I can recollect staying with Aunt Roberta—in the house in the picture. I can also remember something about a litter of puppies being born on the back porch. But I have no memory at all of the big man with the stern face...

In that old snapshot, my face is blurred and out of focus. Yet in my earliest memories, it is *his* face that is a blur—and less than a blur. He simply isn't there at all.

In later years, my mother explained to me that I had a father named Joe Robison, that he lived somewhere else, and that he had a problem. A drinking problem. I didn't understand much as a small boy, but I knew I had been placed in several different homes, and I knew I didn't have a daddy like other boys.

My first real memory of my father is tied to something that happened when I was thirteen. With no permanent address, we were at that time staying in the home of one of Mother's friends. I had been ill for several weeks with some kind of infection and a high, persistent fever. My mother, as a one-time practical nurse, was actually concerned for my life.

She picked up the phone and dialed my father's number, the first time I ever recall such a thing happening. I can still remember her words. "Joe," she said, "if you want to see your son, you'd better come see him now."

I hadn't realized how serious my condition was. Evidently, it was severe enough to bring a mysterious father out of the shadows and back into my life. I remember my mother standing in the doorway, watching for him. Weak and lightheaded as I was, I got up off the couch to stand with her. A car had driven up outside, but it hadn't pulled up along the curb as you would expect. The driver had driven the car *over* the curb, with the front tires in the lawn and the car's back end sticking out into the street.

THE DISTORTED FACE

A man—a tall man—staggered out of the car and shuffled up the sidewalk toward the porch. My mother said quietly, "James, that's your daddy."

My first thoughts were, *I've got a daddy. That's my daddy. That's my father.* But I wondered why he couldn't walk straight.

When I looked into his face I was not impressed with what I saw. He came into the house smelling of whiskey and tobacco, slumped into a chair, and immediately began to curse and boast about himself and his exploits. He barely knew how to say hello. There was no warmth or affection in his face for me—or even much interest. His expression seemed distorted and surly. He looked me up and down for a few seconds with glassy eyes and mumbled something incoherent.

Over the next few days, I thought, *Well, now I've got a dad. Maybe he'll play catch with me.* Football season had just started, and once when we were sitting in the living room I impulsively grabbed a football and tossed it across the room to him. He didn't catch it, but he picked it up off the floor, grabbed it awkwardly on one end, and shoved it back to me. I thought as he threw it, *Good night; the man doesn't even know how to hold a football.*

My daddy didn't know how to hold or throw a ball. He knew how to open a bottle. He knew how to drink.

Several people over the years told me my father was handsome, but I thought he was the ugliest man I'd ever seen. He may have been good-looking in the eyes of others, *but not to me.* When people would tell me how handsome he was, I could not understand how they could be so deceived. I couldn't see any redemptive quality in his face or in his life. He was drunk most of the time. He shuffled and stumbled and couldn't walk straight. He teetered even when he was sober. It hurt me to see him. *This is the man who left me. This is the man who never held me. This is the man who doesn't know how to express his affection because he is consumed by his own selfish pursuits. How could he be anything but ugly?*

I lose track of months—even years—during this period of my life. I think they must have been so dark and unhappy that I tried to block them out of my mind. And I almost succeeded. Truthfully, to bring some of these scenes back, I've had to search and probe my memory—and it has been very painful. But it's strange the things that *do* come back, once you open the rusty gate of abandoned memories.

I remember my father stealing my life savings to buy drinks. It didn't amount to much—maybe seven or eight dollars—but it was all the money I'd ever been able to save. I remember not having hair tonic, because my daddy drank it all—just as he drank everything in the house that might have contained a little alcohol. Even then I remember thinking, *This is a very sick man.*

But the thing I remember most about my father during this period was his face. A face distorted by alcohol. A face with hard and twisted features. A face never once softened by love or compassion or pity. And most of all…a face filled with anger.

THE ANGRY FACE

Eventually, for no reason that I could ever understand, my mother married Joe Robison, my natural father. From that point forward, whatever I had imagined to be hard or difficult in life suddenly seemed like nothing at all. The fires of hell descended on our little home. My father often came home raging drunk. He would curse me and my mother, sometimes becoming violent.

One day when I wasn't home he came in drunk, got his hands

around my mother's throat, and choked her until she passed out on the floor. Mother told me afterward that had she not passed out from lack of oxygen, he would have killed her. As it was, he tossed her aside like a rag doll, thinking she was already dead.

When I came home that night and saw my mother's bruised throat, I remember saying to myself, *If he ever tries that with me, he'll never get away with it.*

As a fourteen-year-old boy with a job in a grocery story, I was allowed to buy and operate a motor scooter. But it wasn't long before I was in a terrible accident that almost killed me. After I recovered from my injuries and the insurance had fixed my scooter, I immediately sold it—out of fear for my life. With the proceeds, I bought a deer rifle, a Model 70 Winchester 30-06. I'd always wanted a father to take me hunting or fishing, or to just do something with me like I knew some dads did. I bought that rifle, dreaming of a day when I might go hunting.

After target-practicing out in the country several times with a friend, I had the rifle in my closet, ammunition close at hand.

That rifle was in the back of my mind as my father came through the front door one day and immediately began cursing me and threatening me. He said he was going to beat me up and—if he felt like it—he might even kill me.

Had he so much as flinched, I would have blown my own father into eternity.

After choking my mother as he had, I believed him. When he threatened me, I ran past him into the hallway, grabbing a baseball bat by the door as I raced toward my bedroom. *If he follows me,* I thought, *I'm going to crush him with this bat.* I could still hear him yelling and raging out in the living room, so I ran to my closet and grabbed my rifle. With shaking hands, and heart pounding in my throat, I shoved in a cartridge and walked back into the living room.

Pointing the Winchester at his chest, I said in the strongest voice I could muster, "If you so much as move your *hand,* I'm going to blow a hole in you big enough for somebody to crawl through!" And I meant it. Had he even raised a hand in fear, I would have blown my own father into eternity. *That's how frightened I was.* (And my life, too, could have been destroyed in that moment of terror.) While he stood there and cursed me, I reached over to the telephone and called the police.

The officer who responded was from the sheriff's department, the same deputy who had helped me after my motor scooter accident. He had liked me, followed up with me, and found out that I'd had a troubled life. So when he heard the dispatcher's call that there was some kind of dispute in the Robison home, he jammed his foot against the accelerator of his patrol car and headed for our place.

Coming through the door he said, "You can put that rifle down, son. I'll take care of this." He put my daddy under arrest and took him off to jail. Thankfully, they were able to keep him there. After running a check, they found out he'd been writing bad checks and using the money to buy liquor.

THE FACE IN THE CASKET

Years after I had become an active young evangelist, speaking in stadiums and coliseums all over America, I went to see my father again. We were holding meetings in a stadium half an hour outside of Austin, near where my father lived in a filthy, run-down little rental house.

"Daddy Joe," I said, "would you come hear me speak? You can come and hear me speak in a stadium with lots of other people. You don't have to dress up. Nobody's going to bother you, or even know you. I'll just be talking about God, Daddy Joe, and I'd like you to come hear me. I'll even pick you up and take you there. Won't you come?"

He nodded his head and told me yes, he would come.

When I came by for him that evening, however, he'd changed his mind—if he'd ever intended to go in the first place. He just looked at me with those vacant eyes and said, "I'm not going, son." So I drove to the stadium alone, my heart heavy in my chest.

The following week I was speaking at Pennington Stadium, near Fort Worth. Six or seven thousand people were coming out every night, and God's presence was very evident. Dr. W. A. Criswell, pastor of the great First Baptist Church, Dallas, even attended and was so complimentary. Afterward he wrote these words:

> Once in a generation a star arises on the spiritual horizon whose beams fall upon uncounted thousands in pristine glory and celestial power. One such star is James Robison. He is an evangelist called of God and his voice is like that of John the Baptist, urging the people to repentance and to faith in Jesus, our Lord.
>
> He is a God-made preacher. The Lord in Heaven bestowed upon him ten talents. All ten he has dedicated fully and completely in the service of the Master. In answer to his appeal, the Holy Spirit bestows many souls. Whether in a church house or in a civic auditorium or in a football stadium, the power and presence of the Lord is upon him.
>
> With infinite gratitude to God for him and his ministry, we are looking forward to the years that lie ahead in which he will be increasingly used by the Holy Spirit to preach the gospel of Christ. No young man has had a greater or more effectual door opened before him than James Robison. God bless him in the great work and God use him to win untold multitudes to the Savior.

On Wednesday morning of that week, I received a phone call. Could I come to my father's funeral on Thursday? He had died in his sleep. My first thought was, *Oh, Daddy, I wish you'd come to that meeting.*

When I first arrived at the funeral home, there was a problem. There weren't enough men to carry the casket. My daddy had lived his whole life and didn't even have a friend. There were only a few of us in the little chapel that afternoon: my mother, my daddy's sister, a couple of other people I didn't recognize, and the pallbearers the funeral home had hastily recruited for the purpose, right off the street.

After the message, I walked by the casket and looked down at my father's face for the last time. A man standing next to me said, "Boy, your father was a good-lookin' man. Real handsome."

I looked down at the big man with the dark, wavy hair and once again found myself thinking, *What are they seeing? How could anybody believe that?* All I could think about was the pain and the dread and the fear and the loss. All I could think about was the grieving little boy who had longed for a daddy with everything that was inside him. But this man had been unavailable. Distant. Cold. He hadn't been there when I needed him. He had been absent for most of my life, and now he was gone forever.

THE FACE IN THE COMIC BOOK

As a young boy, I had always believed there was a God somewhere "out there." At one point I had become marginally involved in a religious group, and had actually been christened. But this had had very little impact on my life. God might really exist, but He didn't have much to do with a shy, lonely boy named James Robison. (Or so I imagined.)

I'd heard people talk about Jesus and "the Father," but somehow it had never seemed real to me. Yet as I look back, I know that my true Father was reaching out to me even then.

Before I was even a teenager, I began working at a grocery store—where I worked for several years. One day as I was walking by the comic book rack, I happened to notice a "Classics Illustrated" comic book on the life of Jesus Christ. It was sitting there next to Superman, Batman, and the Flash, and for some reason, I felt drawn to pick it up.

I flipped it open and *bam!* Something hit me like a bolt of electricity. Standing there by the comic book rack, dressed in a white apron and with a price-marker sticking out of my back pocket, I looked into a full-page picture of Jesus Christ.

I saw His face.

I can still see it today.

It was on a right-hand page. Jesus had just come up out of the water after John the Baptist had baptized Him in the Jordan River. There was a beautiful white dove flying above His head and words were printed in a bright blue comic-book sky...

"This is My beloved Son, in whom I am well pleased."

Something happened in that instant. Something I cannot fully explain, even these many years later. Looking at that face, it was like an arrow had pierced my heart, my conscience, my total being. *Man,* I said to myself. *Man.*

I just stood there, knowing in my heart that no one had ever said those words to me. I had never had a father say he was pleased with me. I'd never had anyone put his hand on my shoulder and say, "You did good, son. I'm proud of you."

How I longed for that! And I thought to myself, *God the Father was pleased with Jesus, with His Son. Boy,...I wonder if God could ever be pleased with me?*

THE FACE THAT SMILED

In my midteens, after the incident with the rifle, I went back to Pasadena, Texas, to stay with the Hale family—the pastor and his wife who had tried to adopt me as a baby, and had been so kind to me. With my father in prison and my mother's life falling to pieces, I just needed to be away for a while, and the Hales welcomed me with open arms.

On the Wednesday night after I arrived, Pastor Hale talked to all the young people at Memorial Baptist Church, asking them to be kind to me and accept me. He also asked the whole congregation to pray for me, explaining that I had been their foster boy when I was little, and that I'd had a hard, troubled life since being taken from their home.

There was a special evangelistic meeting scheduled for Sunday night, and Mrs. Hale asked the whole church to pray for my salvation.

Sitting in a back pew that Sunday night, I listened as Pastor Hale addressed the young people in the audience.

"I want any of our teenagers who would like to share to come up here on the platform and tell what Jesus means to you. Come on up, young people, God bless you. Stand up right where you are and come on up here with me."

I remember thinking, *Well, this won't take long.* Back in Austin, the kids I'd been running with didn't have any time for God. Everyone had to be tough and have a thick shell just to survive. It was hard for me to imagine a group of kids having much to say about Jesus Christ. I honestly didn't think anybody would get up, and was feeling a little bit sorry for Pastor Hale. Then, to my complete surprise, a large group of kids stood and walked to the front. More and more came, until the platform was filled with them. I'd never seen anything like it.

In that moment, for the first time in my life, I heard the voice of my Father.

I leaned forward in my chair as those kids—excited, sharp-looking teens—started talking about loving God and loving Jesus; and they talked about how Jesus was so real in their lives, and how He'd helped them with their problems. They talked about God being their *Father,* and how He was always there for them. In spite of myself (and even though I wanted to look unconcerned and "cool") I felt a lump growing in my throat. I began to really think about what they were saying.

Suddenly I remembered that comic book picture of Jesus, and the thought flashed back into my mind, stronger than ever before—*Could God be pleased with me? If I gave my life to God, would He be pleased with me like He was with Jesus?*

It played on my mind, all the way through Pastor Hale's sermon. In that moment, having the heavenly Father pleased with me, James

Robison, seemed the most important thing in all the world.

As we stood to sing a closing hymn, I heard Pastor Hale saying, "If you want to give your life to God tonight, come take my hand." And I wanted to! Everything in me wanted to. But I felt sick with fear. Shy James Robison was gripping the seat in front of him so hard that his knuckles went white. I couldn't move.

After several verses, I was still standing there, wanting so much to go forward, but stuck in my place as though my feet were encased in cement.

And then I looked up and saw Mrs. Hale, the pastor's wife, coming down the aisle toward me. She was weeping so hard that her glasses kept sliding down her nose. Walking over to where I was standing, holding her glasses in place with one hand, she put her other hand on my shoulder.

"James," she said, "James…don't you want to go to Jesus?"

"Yes, ma'am, but I'm afraid."

"I'll go with you, James. We could go together."

Slowly, and for me courageously, I stepped out into the aisle.

I walked to the front and put my hand in the pastor's hand, but I knew that at the same time I was putting my very life into God's hand. And in that moment, for the first time in my life I really believe I heard the voice of my Father.

He was saying, *I'm pleased, James. You've done well, son. I'm pleased.*

For the first time in memory, I realized I had a Father who approved of me. And suddenly it was as though I had everything I'd wanted and longed for since I was a little boy. I had an encourager. I had approval and acceptance. I had a Friend. I had a Buddy. Pouring into every void in my life, there was a powerful, abiding presence. And through it all, I heard and felt the words I have clung to since that night.

"I am your Father."

If I could have seen the face of this Father, I knew what I would be seeing: a look of approval…and a smile.

A FATHER...AND A BROTHER

I was so excited about what happened to me that when I went back home to Austin a few days later I found my best friend and told him all about it. As we walked at twilight down a well-worn path, through a field and into the woods, I told him how I'd accepted Jesus as my Savior, and how God had become my very own Father. As it turned out, my best friend—who had also grown up without a dad—was the first person I ever led to the Lord.

"James," he said, "I want God as my Father, too."

So he prayed to receive Jesus, and we spent that whole night out in the woods, just talking to our Father.

I remember looking up at the moon as it rose in the late-night sky.

"My Father made that moon," I said.

My friend replied, "*My* Father made that moon, too." That's when it struck him. He looked at me and said, "James, you know...*we've got the same Father now, don't we?*"

Two teenage boys smiled at each other and laid back on the ground, staring up through tree boughs at the moon and stars.

And I think God was smiling at that moment, too. I think there was a smile of approval on our Father's face.

Through the years of young manhood and now into midlife, I have found in Him everything I have ever wanted or missed in a father. He even goes fishing with me, and knows where the big ones are (even though He doesn't always tell me). And in later years, when I became a husband and the father of three precious children, He became the role model and example I'd never known or seen. As a young father, I remember looking down in the darkness at my sleeping children, then kneeling and crying out in my heart, *God, I don't even know how to be a daddy; please help me!*

I have found in Him everything I have ever wanted or missed in a father.

He has helped me. Time after time. In spite of my failures. And even when I would foolishly turn away from His face sometimes and go my own way, He has remained faithful and forgiving. What a Father! And no matter what has happened in your life, no matter where your winding path has led up to this point, He can become to you the Father who is always with you, who is always leading in just the right way…if you will seek His face.

He can make those who have grown up with strong fathers appreciate their role even more, and He can fill every void in the lives of those who missed the positive contributions a good father could have made.

That's His promise. And that, my friend, is the promise of this book.

Chapter Two

A Father Who Is There

Even if my father and mother abandon me,
the LORD will hold me close. [1]

DAVID

N ot long ago, a chaplain in a federal prison had an inspiration. His idea was to help the convicts honor their mothers on Mother's Day. As it happened, a nationally known greeting card company saw an opportunity for a little favorable publicity in the good chaplain's plan, and agreed to furnish cards for all the prisoners who requested them. All an inmate had to do was pick up a card, sign it, and mail it.

The response bowled everyone over—including the ecstatic chaplain. Almost *all* the prisoners, over five hundred men, responded to the offer and mailed the free cards. A gush of poetry and sentiment poured out of that stark, high-walled institution unlike anything anyone had ever seen.

Heartened by the success, the chaplain decided to launch Phase Two. He would do the same thing for Father's Day. Once again, the company furnished cards—enough for every inmate in the facility. The prisoners had only to request them and address them. This time, however, the results were shockingly different.

Not a single inmate requested a card to send his dad. Not even one.

Most of the men incarcerated in that facility either didn't know who their fathers were or had never had enough contact with them to have received much of an impression at all. None of them was interested in sending greetings to a shadowy person he barely knew. It wasn't worth the time to sign a name and lick a stamp.

I was moved by that story. For the inmates, idling away the days and years of their lives behind bars, "Dad" was practically a foreign word. He simply wasn't there for these men, or if he had been, his example had been corrupt—which might help explain why so many of them were where they were. And, but for God's grace, their stories could so easily have been mine.

Many are scarred for life by the hurt and loneliness of a father's absence.

Fortunately, not every man or woman who grows up without a good father ends up in jail (or else I would be writing this book right now from a cell block). But many are scarred for life by the hurt and loneliness of a father's absence. It has become such a universal problem in our culture that if you have actually enjoyed a meaningful relationship with your father, you are particularly blessed and have a heritage many would deeply envy.

Because I never had the opportunity to enjoy the company of my own father, I was sure it would be different for me when I had children. And for the most part, it has been. My adult children and I have warm, close relationships to this day, and we share a wealth of fun and happy memories.

One of my most treasured possessions is a framed enlargement of my son Randy and I out on a lake in a bass boat. Randy was about fourteen at the time, and while we were fishing, just after a red setting sun had slipped behind the trees, my sweet wife snapped our picture. I've named that framed photograph "Tranquillity," and it reminds me of wonderful moments I've been privileged to enjoy with my three children through the years—moments that now shine like pure gold in my memory.

I look so relaxed, so at peace in that picture. Yet there was a time, early in my marriage, when I found myself walking very close to the danger zone as a father, and I didn't even realize it.

RIDING THE WAVE

There were days and weeks when the demands of my evangelistic ministry seemed so intense I wondered how I would keep on top of it all. City after city. Crusade after crusade. Stadium after stadium. It was like riding a huge wave that was rolling me forward and breaking all around me. You not only couldn't go back, you couldn't stay in one place and tread water. It was either advance or drown!

In those days, I was speaking in high schools all over America to thousands of teens during the day, and at arenas packed with families in the evening. And there's no doubt about it, the opportunities were exciting. Thousands of people were coming to Christ or rededicating their lives, and we were seeing dramatic evidence of changed lives and changed communities.

But I had another little flock, back in Texas, that I wasn't seeing as much of as I would have liked: My wife, Betty, and my little three-year-old daughter, Rhonda.

In one of my brief stopovers at home, an understanding pastor I'd been ministering with that week called me one morning and said, "Spend the day with your family, James. We've got things to do here, but we can take care of 'em."

"Well—if you're sure," I said, "then thank you. I believe I will."

So I did something that day I hadn't done in a good long while. I let Betty have some well-deserved time to herself while I spent the *whole* day just playing with my little girl. And what a time we had! The day was filled with laughter, chatter, silly games, animal cookies, and hugs galore.

Late that afternoon, before Betty got home, I left Rhonda with her coloring book in the den and slipped back into my bedroom for some time alone with the Lord. Pulling the door shut, I got down on my knees by the bed. As I look back, I'm not really sure why I shut that door. Did I have some feelings of reticence or reluctance about my little daughter seeing me pray? How foolish. Our children *need* to see their mamas and daddies on their knees.

As it happened, the closed door didn't matter much anyway. Rhonda felt she had proprietary rights on her daddy that day, and didn't want to let me stray too far out of her sight. I heard the door push open behind me, and little feet padding on the carpet.

She came over to where I was kneeling, stood there a moment, and just patted me on the shoulder.

"You sure are a sweet daddy," she said. Then she turned around and walked back out of the room.

That really touched my heart. I've always had a strong, forceful personality, and most people seemed to think of me as tough, stern, maybe even harsh at times. So I had been described in a lot of different ways—but I'd never before heard anyone call me "sweet." My eyes teared up a little as I knelt there, and I told the Lord, "Well, God, I guess You're the only One who can make me sweet."

Dear Jesus . . . please help my daddy to play with me more.

In a minute or two, the door opened again and Rhonda came back into the room. This time she knelt down beside me and said, "I want to pray too, Daddy."

"Well, sure, Honey," I said. "Daddy would like for you to pray. You go ahead and talk to Jesus."

In her clear, piping little voice, Rhonda said, "Dear Jesus, thank you for Mommy, thank you for Daddy, and thank you for Rhonda, too." I smiled at the tenderness of the moment. But what she said next broke my heart.

"*And dear Jesus,*" my little girl prayed, "*please help my daddy to play with me more.*"

It was like a dagger in my chest.

I was touching the lives of hundreds and thousands of young people across our great country…but one little girl back in Texas just needed a daddy to play with. And I was the only daddy she had.

Since my grandchildren have come along, and I've had opportunities to observe the choice little things they're learning and doing, it recently struck me that I don't remember hardly any of those little actions or expressions in the lives of my own children. I'm sure they did and said the same sorts of cute and amazing things when they were babies and toddlers, but too often I wasn't around to witness those things.

I would be staying in some distant city and see a six- or seven-year-old child, and just be hit by the fact that I'd probably been around my children less than half of their lives. In retrospect, I know that I traveled more than I really needed to. I could have worked smarter and stayed home more. But in the zeal of the moment—in my zeal for the Lord—I neglected some things I now realize God never intended for me to neglect.

NO GREATER GIFT

A father has no greater gift to give his children than time.

You've heard that before. It's nothing new. But how long has it been since the truth of that statement just reached out and gripped your heart? When you are long gone and your children are grown and sitting on a front porch or a back deck somewhere on a summer night, just watching the fireflies, what will they remember when they look back across their lives? The trendy clothes? The dolls and games? The big-name basketball shoes? The computers and CD players? The cars? The big house?

No, I don't think those are the sorts of things men and women tend to remember under the summer stars. What they will remember in those quiet moments will be those times when you, their only daddy, pushed other priorities to one side—even at risk to your career or personal interests—and just made time to *be there*. With them. Hear the words of a man who has spent countless hours with young men and women from one end of our country to another: Earning extra money for extra things *isn't even in the same ballpark* with being there and being available to your sons and daughters.

You'd think those of us in full-time ministry who work with so many wounded people and families in crisis would have that fact pretty well nailed down. Yet all too often we get so caught up with everyone else's struggles and needs that we hurry right past hurting people on our way out the front door.

Some time ago, I heard about a Christian conference speaker who had planned a fishing trip with his boy. They'd made plans: which lakes they were going to hit, what bait they would use, where they would camp, and what "good stuff" they'd take along for meals and snacks. The boy had his gear all packed days in advance.

But one evening, the man got a long-distance call and had to make a quick decision. He was being asked to fill in for someone at the last moment at a very large and prestigious gathering on the very day he and his boy had planned to be away together. How could he say no? It was not only an impressive career opportunity, it offered *a thousand dollar honorarium*—a greater stipend than he'd ever received.

"Son," he explained to his boy, "I can't do the fishing trip this weekend. I sure planned to, and wanted to, but I just have to take this engagement. You understand that, don't you?" When his disappointed boy didn't say anything, the father felt moved to an act of what he thought was extraordinary generosity.

"I'll tell you what I'm going to do, son. I'm going to *split* that honorarium with you, since I can't be here with you. That's five hundred dollars for you, Buddy. Think of what you could do with that."

The little boy looked at him and shrugged. "That's all right, Dad. You just keep the money. You're worth more to me than a thousand dollars will ever be."

That little guy's statement just underlines the truth one more time: The greatest thing you can do for your children, apart from leading them to Jesus Christ and praying for them daily, is to find ways to invest time in their lives. Period. A child can recognize that a dad's busy with all manner of things at any given moment, and will actually measure his or her own importance and value on the basis of how that father decides to use his time. Whether you want it to happen or not, your child will wonder, *How do I stack up alongside Dad's business, job, hobbies, or mission in life? How do I rate on his scale of "important things"? Am I in the top three? The top ten? Or am I there at all?*

THE INVISIBLE MAN

Sometimes, at the most unexpected moments, a man can gain an instant of clarity and perspective. It's as though the heavy clouds suddenly and unexpectedly part, allowing a shaft of pure sunlight to illuminate a portion of landscape he hasn't seen for a while. Oliver Wendell Holmes once wrote: "A moment's insight is sometimes worth a life's experience."

Ken Canfield speaks of such a moment when he was working late at the office one night and called home. His little girl happened to answer the phone, and after greeting her, Ken said, "Now would you get Mommy to come to the phone, please?" He heard his little girl shout to the next room, "Mom, it's for you. It's the Invisible Man."

At first he smiled at the reference, but then the words struck home…and began to burn in his conscience. As he sat there in the quiet of his office that night, waiting for his wife to come to the phone, he thought to himself, "I guess she's right. As far as she's concerned, I *have* been the invisible man."

In that small moment of clarity, he caught a glimpse of his life—as though he were somehow above himself looking down. How had he become an invisible man to his daughter? He could see himself running here and there, leaving for work before dawn, staying after hours, catching planes, hurrying to endless meetings…and suddenly he knew in his heart that every one of his achievements and conquests at work paled in comparison to being there for that little girl.[2]

KNOWING YOUR CHILDREN

Some time after the 1995 bombing of the Oklahoma City federal building, I remember watching the accused bomber's father being interviewed on network television. The reporter's questions were rather simple and straightforward, asking the older man about his son's interests and concerns and plans in life. Yet all that poor, bewildered father could do was shake his head time after time and say, "I don't know…I have no idea…I couldn't tell you…I just couldn't say."

It became painfully obvious that the man didn't know his son at all, and had probably *never* known him. He may have cared for his son, and they may have lived eighteen years together under the same roof, but he had no idea what was in the young man's heart and soul. Was his son capable of such a horrendous act? You might as well have asked a stranger, because this father just didn't know.

It's so tragic that fathers do not know their children beyond a shallow, superficial depth. It seems that so few men ever take the opportunity to really delve into their sons' and daughters' interests, fears, hopes, and dreams. Then years later, when they're standing around together at some family reunion, everyone feels strained and awkward and no one knows what to talk about. Why? Because they have never really known one another. They've never made the effort.

When you think about it, most kids aren't asking for the world. All they want is that minimum amount of time that will allow them to feel that dad is really on their team. That he's interested in them and cares about them. Kids don't expect their fathers to be all-wise and have all the answers. They just want dad to be there, to give them a little time, to show them some consistent affection; they need to see that dad is willing to help them work through some of their problems.

THE FATHER WHO IS THERE

It hurts to remember those times when we longed for a father to be there in those special or lonely moments of our lives, yet he wasn't there. If I thought much about those memories, I could easily begin to weep at this moment as I write these words. The emotions are still that close to the surface, even though I'm now in my fifties, and have nine grandchildren. But the truth is, even though I didn't grow up with a daddy who was always there, I *found* such a Father in God.

He is with me in a way no earthly father could ever be, no matter how close and loving the relationship.

Just what kind of father is He?

HE'S AN EVERLASTING FATHER

Even if we're the best and wisest dad in the land, we're only temporary employees in this business of parenthood. Our job as father is mostly over when our children reach adulthood. The major portion of the guidance and instruction must be administered within a period of about eighteen years. After that, our role in our children's lives changes. At that point, we're no longer the authority figure we once were; we serve only in an advisory capacity. We no longer have that close supervision over the development of our children, and we have little or no control over their behavior.

God actually planned it this way, ordaining that a man "leave his father and his mother" when he becomes mature enough to marry and begin his own family.

But God continues to be a Father throughout life in this world and on into eternity to those who are born spiritually into His family. Scripture calls Him the "Everlasting Father."[3] He will always "be there" for us and our kids! Even after we're only a memory down here on earth, the Everlasting Father will walk with them step for step through all their days.

THE EVER-PRESENT FATHER

Even during those approximately eighteen years that a child is in the home with his earthly father, he is actually in the presence of that father for only two or three hours a day—at most! During those few hours, he has his father's attention only briefly. One study indicates that American fathers who remain with their families spend an average of only twenty minutes a day actually engaging in conversation or doing something with their children.

But God never leaves His children—and they are His children no matter how young or old they might be! God once said to the people of Israel, "Listen to me.... I created you and have cared for you since before you were born. I will be your God throughout your lifetime—until your hair is white with age. I made you, and I will care for you. I will carry you along and save you."[4]

He is constantly present with His children, and not just for a few minutes in the evening! We have His undivided attention every minute of our lives. As David wrote, His thoughts toward us are more numerous than the grains of sand that cover the earth.[5] When you look at life in its totality, a child does relatively few things with his natural father. But *everything* a child of God does he does with his heavenly Father.

We have His undivided attention every minute of our lives.

David told the Lord, "You have been my refuge, a strong tower against the foe."[6] He is a like a high tower that enables us to see danger from some distance away. That's what a high tower is for, isn't it? You're in an elevated position of safety and security, and you can see any kind of trouble when it first comes over the horizon. In our national forests, rangers man observation towers high atop hills and ridges. From such vantage points, they can spot the first column of smoke that signals a potentially dangerous forest fire.

The presence of the Lord in our lives is like that. He's up in that tower scanning the horizons of our life. He knows our past, our present, and our future. As we walk with Him, He warns us and teaches us and points out the best path. As a loving, patient Father, He's on the alert for us, He's looking out for us.

AN INTERESTED FATHER

It was so moving to realize that I have a Father who is interested in what interests me. He always seems to care about what's on my mind. He probes. He asks questions. He knows the desires of my heart and cares about them.

In one of his songs, David said of the Lord, "The LORD is close to all who call upon him, yes, to all who call on him sincerely. He fulfills the desires of those who fear him."[7]

I've said I always wanted a father to take me fishing and hunting, and it seemed to me that as I really let God be a Father to me, He had all kinds of activities planned. Who knows where the exciting outdoor adventures are better than He? Who knows better where the big fish like to school? Who knows where the deer browse? Who knows every rock and tree and deep pool and game trail and breathtaking landscape on this planet? God, my heavenly Father. There is no One like Him.

Through the years, in His kindness to me, He has arranged for me to speak in Alaska or Canada or other wonderful wilderness areas. And every now and then He's brought licensed guides into my meetings, and men who seemingly couldn't wait to take me out salmon fishing or bear hunting or whatever. And in those times, I've sensed my Father's smile. I've heard Him say, "See, James? I knew what you longed for as a boy growing up. Remember, I know the desires of your heart, and I love you."

Early in my ministry, before I'd had much opportunity to go fishing, I remember a series of meetings out in east Texas. After one of the meetings, who should walk up and introduce himself but the number one fishing guide on Sam Rayburn Lake. During my time there in that community, he took me out in his boat several times and showed me things I'd never seen before. On one of my first casts, I remember throwing out a top-water lure and having two large bass hit that lure

He is a Father with a limitless capacity to comfort.

from different sides at the same instant. Talk about fun! I got so excited, I about fell out of the boat. And I can remember thinking in my heart, "Boy, *God* did this for me. I'm on a real fishing trip today with my Father."

The fact is, He cares about what I care about and never takes my heart's desires lightly. David realized the same thing when he wrote, "Take delight in the LORD, and he will give you your heart's desires."[8]

Sometimes earthly fathers and mothers put pressure on a son or daughter to fulfill their own unfulfilled dreams and aspirations— whether the child truly is inclined the way the parent is or not. That puts a heavy, sometimes intolerable, strain on a young man or young woman. Father God, however, cares about *my* dreams and *your* dreams. However grandiose or however small they may be, however silly or inconsequential they may seem to others, our dreams are important to our heavenly Father. If your dream is a house with a little white picket fence around it and children playing in the yard, God shares that dream with you. He cares about what's in your heart. And if somehow that dream doesn't seem to be realized in a certain time frame, He is there to comfort you and see you through.

He's the One who can wait with you. He's the One who makes waiting not only possible and endurable, but actually a pleasant experience. He is a Father with a limitless capacity to comfort.[9]

A FATHER WHO WAITS FOR US

I remember so well being in Bible college not long after I'd accepted Jesus as my Savior. I explored the countryside around the college until I found a beautiful pine woods, where I would retreat just to walk and talk with God. I told my Father how much I loved Him and wanted to serve Him. I thanked Him for calling me to preach and for giving me a boldness that wasn't only above and beyond what I could have mustered, but also went against the very grain of my shy personality.

I went back into that woods nearly every day, eager to tell the Lord how much I loved Him. His presence saturated the atmosphere—I don't know how else to explain it. He seemed to say, "I've been waiting for you. I love you so much, James." I felt like I could reach up and take Him by the hand and walk with Him. It was that clear to me. The joy of finally having a father to talk to—a father who cared so deeply about me—filled my heart until I thought it would burst.

Some time later, when I'd fallen away from that simple, joyful walk with the Father, I thought about my little place in the woods and went back. And once again, I just had the overwhelming sense that in some way I can't even describe, God the Father had been waiting for me through those days and weeks when I never came. That even though I hadn't been faithful to our meeting time and our meeting place, He had never missed a day. And it just pierced my heart to realize that.

Big as I am, I'm not too big or too old for this Father's lap.

I remember another season of time, not all that long ago, when I hadn't been praying or reading the Bible or seeking my Father's face. It wasn't calculated. It wasn't deliberate. It wasn't rebellion. I'd just gotten myself overly busy and frazzled, and in spite of good intentions, my time with the Lord dwindled and dwindled until the fellowship wasn't there anymore.

I remember late one evening, tired as I was, picking up my Bible and sitting down in my recliner. As I laid my head back against the cushion, I sighed deeply and suddenly found myself talking to God again.

"Father," I said, "I've been busy and preoccupied. I guess I haven't talked to You much or had much time for You, have I?"

And in that moment I had the most overwhelming sense that I was a child sitting on a lap, resting my head on the strong shoulder of the most powerful being in the universe. There I was, a middle-aged father and grandfather, resting on God's lap.

He seemed to be saying to me, "I've missed you, son." He didn't scold me. He didn't get after me about neglecting Him and not seeking Him. He just told me how glad He was to see me. I found myself weeping. Just to think that He—the heavenly Father—had *missed* me!

And in that moment, He held me.

Big as I am, I'm not too big or too old for this Father's lap and shoulder.

And neither are you.

Chapter Three

A Father Who Listens

*I love the LORD because he hears
and answers my prayers.
Because he bends down and listens,
I will pray as long as I have breath!*[1]

THE PSALMS

O
ver twenty years ago, some enterprising soul placed the following tiny ad in the classified section of a large Kansas daily: *"I will listen to you talk for thirty minutes without a comment for $5."*

It was no hoax. The individual set up shop and soon had all the customers he could handle. People scattered across the wide Kansas prairies were so lonely they were willing to try anything for a half-hour of companionship.[2]

I'd be willing to bet that ad was placed before the explosion of "talk radio" in our culture. Now you can find a listening ear—or maybe a couple of million of them—for practically nothing.

Have you ever been driving at night and scanned the AM radio dial? The airwaves these days are full of talk. Even in the wee hours of the morning you can hear men and women across the continent spilling out their hopes and dreams and fears to a faceless "voice" in the night. A trucker rolling along the interstate speculates into his cell phone about the fortunes of his favorite football team. A young mother in a high-rise apartment tells of her hurt and loneliness to whomever might care to listen. A nurse on the night shift at a large hospital uses her break to share a few opinions about local politics—and about doctors, too.

The talk goes on and on, seven days a week, twenty-four hours a day. *We've become a nation of talkers in search of listeners.*

I've often speculated that for every one hundred talkers in the world, there may only be one or two people with the gift of listening. You might say that talkers are a dime a dozen. You can get "talk" most everywhere you go. If you don't get your fill of it on the radio and still hunger for a human voice, you might wander over to a used car lot and look interested in a '78 Bonneville for about ten seconds. Talk and talkers aren't all that hard to find, but true, compassionate *listeners* are like a handful of rare and precious gems in a truckload of river gravel.

Have you ever found yourself in conversation with a genuine listener? It's amazing how enjoyable it can be! They're so responsive, so appreciative, so attentive, so tuned-in, that you feel like you could go on for hours. On the other hand, it's as disheartening as can be when you have something exciting and important to tell someone and you get the distinct impression they're only "tolerating" you to be polite. They aren't really interested, they're only waiting for an opportunity to speak their own piece. Or to make their escape.

Have you ever tried to converse with someone whose eyes are roving around the room? They may be looking in your general direction, but their attention seems focused on something over your left shoulder somewhere. After a while, you want to grab them by the shoulders and say, "Hey! Are you LISTENING to me?" Some people will say, "Sure, I'm listening," and can repeat back what you said for the last two minutes verbatim. But if they're not looking at you and don't seem responsive to what you're saying, you don't feel *heard.* After all, you don't want a parrot or a Dictaphone, *you want a listener!*

THE ROUND AFTER THE ROUND

Most golfers I know like to talk about their favorite pastime. Through the years, I've found that golf is the most enjoyable outdoor recreation

I participate in. The exercise is beneficial and the competitive aspect makes every single shot important, whether you're playing against someone else, or just competing against your best previous score.

Often, when I've golfed alone and completed a round, I like to call someone and tell 'em how I did. If you ever receive such a call from a golfer, you should know the proper etiquette. The appropriate first question to ask in such a conversation is not, "What did you shoot?" The proper phrasing of that question ought to be, "What do you think you *should* have shot?" That's because most golfers hate to report a bare, unadorned score. Instead, they appreciate the opportunity to add an explanation or two before they get to that bottom line. They like to set the context for their score, to explain the bad bounces and breaks—the "if onlys."

They'll say something like: "Well, I *would have* had par on the sixth hole," or "I *should have* had a birdie on the ninth," or "I *might have* done thus and so, but there was a tornado (or a tidal wave or a herd of caribou) that passed through right in the middle of the game."

I have a few friends who share my passion for trying to control that little white ball, and we like to compare notes now and then. Oftentimes I'll call them after I get home, and not only tell them the score but give them an instant replay of every hole and every shot. That's what's so great about the sport: You can go into wonderful detail about your strokes, the conditions of the course, where your ball landed each time, and what happened with your emotions through every drive, slice, chip, and putt. It's a marvelous release—almost as much fun as the game itself.

This only works, however, when you know the person on the other end of the line really cares about your golf game as much as you do. If you get dead silence on the line for half a minute, or if you notice a series of mechanical "uh-huhs," you can pretty well figure that the individual really doesn't care and would rather be off the phone and doing something (anything!) else.

SOMEONE TO LISTEN

When the Lord created us in His image, He placed within us the capacity to speak and listen. After God paraded all the animals of creation before Adam, the prototype man, the Bible says that "there was no companion suitable for him."[3] As God mused on that fact, He said, "It is not good for the man to be alone. I will make him a companion who will help him."[4] Adam had told the giraffe about his golf game, but the giraffe didn't seem interested. Adam had told the ostrich about what kind of day he'd had, and about his commute through the Garden, but the ostrich gave him no eye contact and didn't say a thing.

But then God created a woman from Adam's side, and presto! He had conversation as he'd never had it before! And it wasn't just chatter. For the first time in the history of the young planet, two human beings shared their words and their very souls—just as the Creator had intended—and it was truly awesome.

Something deep within us longs to be listened to.

Something deep within us longs to be listened to. If no one ever listens or pays attention to us, it's as though something within us begins to wither and die. It is so vital to know that there is someone who really cares about those things that weigh on our hearts and play at the edges of our minds, regardless of the subject matter. Sometimes we find ourselves wondering, *Does anyone care how I feel? Does anyone really care about what I think? Will someone listen carefully enough to hear not only my words, but my heart?*

As a boy, I can well remember wishing I had someone to talk to who really cared about my personal interests—especially those related to outdoor activities. In one of the places where I lived with my mother, there was a little lake nearby where I could go sit on a pier and fish for perch. Catching those feisty little fellas was some of the most fun I'd ever had—but how I wished someone could be with me! I wanted someone to care about the "one that got away," about how many I'd been able to catch—and I mean *really* care. How I longed for someone to talk to about fishing, someone who could understand and share my excitement.

But in those years, there was no one.

There were other times when I just wanted to tell somebody how lonely I felt. From age five to fifteen, my mother and I moved somewhere between ten and fifteen times. I actually lost count. We were very poor, and some of the areas we moved into were rough and hard.

On one occasion, when I was seven or eight years old, we lived in the back part of a motel. My mother served as maid for the entire complex. It certainly wasn't the worst place we'd lived; at least it had a bathroom. But the problem was, we moved there right in the middle of the fall school term. I'd just gotten to know a few kids at the last school, cautiously building a couple of friendships, and I had to leave them behind. Starting over (again) wasn't easy. I remember how lonely and frightening it was to get on the school bus in that neighborhood for the first time with a bunch of hard-faced kids who were strangers. Suddenly, there was no one to talk to. No one cared a lick about a new boy named James Robison. No one knew or understood that sick, empty feeling inside me, or how desperately I missed my friends.

COMMUNICATIONS 101

Riding in my daughter and son-in-law's Suburban along with their four kids makes for an engaging—and sometimes humorous—communications laboratory. Terry and Rhonda's kids—ages ten, six, four, and two—have Robison blood flowing in their veins, which means they are very expressive. At any given moment, they're *all* competing for their mom and dad's immediate attention. Their persistence continually amazes me. Only Lora, the oldest, seems to realize she needs to wait for a moment of silence before trying to wedge a word in edgewise. But Luke, Lincoln, and Laney keep chirping away like little birds in the nest: "Mama! Mama! Daddy! Daddy!" When they realize they're not getting through, they redouble their efforts, pitching their little voices higher and stronger with each attempt.

Daddy or Mama, of course, are trying valiantly to finish a thought with Betty or me, or perhaps one another. Working hard just to com-

The heart cry behind the words...may be even more important.

plete a sentence or two, they deliberately tune out the chorus from the back seats. This is understandable when it comes in the midst of an almost never-ending call and cry for attention. Finally, the parents will try to single out a voice to make a reply. On occasion, I'll even take up one of the children's cause, saying, "You know, ol' Luke here has been trying to say something for about ten minutes..."

It's not that Terry and Rhonda are disinterested in their children's concerns. Far from it. They're just trying to teach the little ones a few ground rules of conversation—such as how to exercise a little patience and wait their turn.

I have heard of occasions, however, when boys or girls call out to their parents and are *never* recognized. After months and even years of being ignored, cut off, or put off, these children will simply stop trying and become silent and withdrawn. And that's sad.

I know there were a few occasions as our own children grew up when I was so preoccupied, heedless, or hurried that I just didn't hear the words of our son or daughters. Or perhaps I heard the words but didn't hear the heart cry *behind* the words—which may be even more important.

THE GOD WHO LISTENS

As I came to know God the Father in a personal way, He taught me to understand how much He truly cares. At first, it seemed too good to be true. Could anyone (especially someone as important and busy as God) really be that concerned about my words, or interested in my thoughts and feelings? *Could it be?* As the truth began to dawn on me, I realized that He not only tolerated my words, He welcomed them with great joy.

He actually wanted to hear me and be with me! This was a Father who liked me to tell Him how I felt.

There's an old gospel song that says, "Now, let us have a little talk with Jesus, let us tell Him all about our troubles. He will hear our earnest cry, and He will answer by and by." That's more than a foot-stomping, rhythmic chorus. It really is the truth. We *can* tell Him our troubles. He *will* hear our earnest cry, because as the psalmist said, when we lift our voices and cry out to Him, He will actually incline His ear toward us. It's a picture of a caring daddy leaning down to hear his child speak. You can imagine a father squatting down to be at eye level with a little one who has been tugging at his pants leg and has something to say.

He is leaning over the edge of heaven to catch your every word.

I believe God not only wants us to share our hearts with Him, but He wants very much for us to count on the fact that He is "all ears." Somehow, though there are millions of voices crying out to Him in every language from all over the world, He focuses His undivided attention on you and me.

You can talk to God as your Father and find in Him someone who genuinely concerns Himself with every point of interest and all the intimate details of your life. This is a Father who invites an open discussion of your anxieties, your pain, your concerns, and the areas of weakness and defeat in your life. He will not shame you. He will direct you, encourage you, and give you strength. He will guide you and walk with you through the valley of the shadow of death, and any other difficulty. He will provide a bright light for your path, and help you walk through those difficult moments. As the apostle James once told a group of suffering believers: "If you don't know what you're doing, pray to the Father. He loves to help. You'll get his help, and won't be condescended to when you ask for it. Ask boldly, believingly, without a second thought."[5]

You will find that He is, in fact, leaning over the edge of heaven to catch your every word, every inflection, and every thought you can't even put into words. He will hear your faintest cry, and He will answer by and by.

ARE YOU LISTENING, GOD?

If anyone had a right to feel that God had stopped listening to him, it was David. Anointed for the kingship of Israel at the tender age of sixteen, he spent most of the next *fifteen years* of his life on the run from the murderous jealousy of King Saul. Hounded from one end of the

This is a Father who knows how to sort through our jumbled thoughts and emotions.

land to the other, he was forced to hide in the loneliest, most desolate corners of the wilderness. At other times, he found himself crawling through a network of midnight black limestone caves to escape the spears of Saul's army.

His reputation was in shambles. He'd been lied about and maligned. Those who might have cared about him were intimidated into withdrawing their friendship and support. He saw no end to his fugitive status. All he had to cling to was a promise he'd received from the prophet Samuel as a young teenager.

Where was God in all of this? If I'd been David, I might have imagined that the phone lines to heaven were down. Or that God had given me a wrong number. Yet somehow, through all those lean, dark, lonely years, David became more convinced than ever that God was listening to him and had heard him.

Listen to these entries from this young man's personal journal:

The ropes of death surrounded me; the floods of destruction swept over me. The grave wrapped its ropes around me; death itself stared me in the face. But in my distress I cried out to the LORD; yes, I prayed to my God for help. *He heard me from his sanctuary; my cry reached his ears....*

In sudden fear I had cried out, "I have been cut off from the Lord!" But *you heard my cry* for mercy and answered my call for help....

This poor man called, and *the LORD heard him*; he saved him out of all his troubles....

I waited patiently for the LORD to help me, and *he turned to me and heard my cry.* He lifted me out of the pit of despair, out of the mud and the mire. He set my feet on solid ground and steadied me as I walked along....

O you who hear prayer, to you all men will come. When we were overwhelmed by sins, you forgave our transgressions.[6]

This is a Father who hears our words and hears us even when we don't have any words. He knows how to sort through our jumbled thoughts and all the cross-currents of our emotions. Paul speaks of God's Spirit as the great "Searcher of hearts."[7]

God always has time for His kids.

He bends down to listen. He gives us eye contact. He pays attention to every word. He remembers everything, even the fact that we're only weak human beings made out of dust.

Busy? Yes, He has a trillion galaxies to run, countless angels to administrate, and a rebellious planet called earth filled with foolish, obstinate people trying to destroy themselves.

But He always has time for His kids.

He *will* listen to you and He will care. And He can teach us to listen to others and care for them as He does. We all need to know someone listens and hears what is in the heart...and cares.

Chapter Four

A Father Who
Talks to Me

*I will instruct you and train you in the way you shall go;
I will counsel you with My eye on you.* [1]

Having no father to talk to me and give direction in my life as a boy, I was left with some tendencies and habits that have caused me concern through the years.

Frankly, I have some blind spots in my life—some insecurities that surface from time to time—and I struggle with them. Could an attentive father have enabled me to identify and deal with those troubling areas in my personality?

Yes, I believe so. And for this reason: I do not see the same weaknesses in my own children that I experienced as a boy. I remember being amazed as I attended school functions with my children and observed the *confidence* with which they moved among their fellow students. I saw security, stability, assurance, and the ability to express themselves so freely and fluently.

How different it was for me. On those rare occasions when I had worked up courage to attend some school function, I would feel alone, out of place, and intimidated by everyone around me.

Psychologists, sociologists, and others who study such things have pointed out again and again how influential the father's influence can be in a child's character development. He has an incalculable impact—

for good or ill—on the formation of a young man or woman's personality, habits, and practices. Without denigrating or minimizing the mother's vital role in parenting, studies have shown that it is the father who leads the way in shaping a child's sense of security, sexual identity, and the capacity to demonstrate respect for the lives and property of others.

A father's voice of authority and guidance have stunning potential for good in the life of a child.

APPLES OF GOLD

Perhaps remembering how my own father had belittled and cursed me (when he was even around), I wanted to take every opportunity to build positive things into the lives of my own three children.

Solomon once said, "The right word spoken at the right time is as beautiful as gold apples in a silver bowl."2 And as the kids and I would spend time together in various activities, I would actively look for opportunities to drop a few of those shiny golden apples into our conversations. I tried to find words that would highlight their strengths and express appreciation for the developing qualities in their lives. I wanted them to believe that, with the Lord's help, they could accomplish anything in life they set their hearts and minds to do.

As it happened, all three of them became student body leaders and honor students, and they each participated in school organizations and activities. And now they're strong parents and spouses, bringing up their own children with a steady hand. I'm so thankful for the shaping role God allowed me to have in their lives. Considering my own background and role models, it was truly a miracle of His grace and kindness.

Looking back, I can remember specific conversations where I tried to insert an encouraging word or comment at the appropriate time.

When our oldest daughter Rhonda was twelve and in junior high school, her physical development was noticeably lagging behind that of some of her friends. One day, as we were driving home after I picked her up at school, I took the risk of broaching that sensitive subject.

"Rhonda," I said, "I know that a lot of your friends have developing figures—and you don't yet. You may wonder about that. But you don't need to. You just need to understand that it's all going to change before you know it. I don't ever want you to worry about it or feel self-conscious."

We rode together in silence for a moment, then I said, "Why don't we just pray?"

So as we drove down those familiar roads toward home, I prayed that God would help her to have confidence and patience. And I prayed that she would fill out in a lovely young woman's figure as she grew up.

In fact, she did! She blossomed into such a beautiful, full-figured woman that our younger daughter seemed a little alarmed by it all. She commented in fun as a seventh grader, "Mom, please tell Daddy not to pray for me like he did for Rhonda!"

On another occasion, I recall a conversation while walking with my son. He was reaching his dating years, and I knew that relationships with girls would soon be a concern to him—if they weren't already.

"Randy," I asked him, "do you want to know how to find the girl who'll be the very best girl possible for your life?"

He gave me a quick sideways glance. "Well...sure, Dad."

"Then just be cool, son. Don't be on the prowl. Be sensitive, be polite, keep your eyes open and your manners and expressions confident. If you stay relaxed and confident—not allowing yourself to become overanxious or in a hurry—girls will be attracted to you. Eventually, as God's will is manifest, you'll find the girl of your choice and you'll have a wonderful life."

And that's exactly what happened. He married the most wonderful girl. Randy says Debbie is much like his mother, whom he greatly admires.

You simply can't overestimate the power of an appropriate, confidence-building affirmation dropped into a child's life at just the right time! And how can you be sure of being there at that "right moment"? The answer is simple, but the outworking of that answer will *never* be simple: Spend all the time you can with your children—even at the expense of your career, your hobbies, and your ministry outside the home.

A FATHER WHO FILLS THE GAP

As I grew up, I missed those affirming times with a father. I didn't get "apples of gold in bowls of silver." It was more like ducking rotten apples! But I can honestly tell you that all the longing and lack in my

You simply can't over-estimate the power of an appropriate affirmation dropped in at the right time in a child's life!

life has been filled with a warm, walking, talking relationship with Almighty God, who has become a dear personal Friend and Father to me in the truest sense of those words.

People have said to me from time to time, "James, you seem to be able to hear God's voice in a special way. You talk about conversing with God as you would about leaning over the back fence to talk to a neighbor. I just don't hear God speak the way you do."

No, not everyone will. But I believe with all my heart that every believer *can*. In fact, God told a prophet of old that if we seek Him with all of our heart we will find Him. In my life, missing my own father's voice as I did, I so hungered for conversation with my heavenly Father that I have pursued and pursued it. And as I did, I found that He had been pursuing *me* and calling me all along.

He loves to talk to me, and I love conversing with Him. It is the joy of my life. And I want to assert and affirm that we can, in fact, hear God talk to us as a loving Father. He *will* communicate His mind, His heart, His will, and His purpose. He *will* give direction and guidance to our lives.

We should all be inspired to initiate communication with our Father, who is so anxious for us to hear and know His voice.

The Bible illustrates this glorious possibility of hearing God's voice from cover to cover. Adam walked and talked with God in the Garden. Abraham conversed openly with God. Isaac, Jacob, Moses, and Joshua heard God's voice, as did the prophets. David, the shepherd-king, heard Him, as did his son Solomon. The disciples learned to hear Him, even after Jesus returned to the Father. Even Peter clearly heard the voice of God's Holy Spirit. The Bible closes with the "revelation," God speaking to mankind through His servant John, showing us all what is "yet to come."

Jesus said that His sheep know His voice.[3] He also said that men must live by "...every word that comes from the mouth of God."[4] God still speaks today as a loving Father. We can learn to know and hear His voice.

No, listening for God's voice is not a matter of trying to hear audible sounds. Most of us will never hear that deep bass voice that spoke to Charlton Heston up on the mountain in *The Ten Commandments*. God could certainly speak in an audible voice if He desired, and there are those who say they've experienced it. But for me, His voice is more profound than that. It's more like a deep spiritual impression on my mind. There are times when I feel it starting in my toes and coming up through my body. When He speaks to me, everything is energized; His voice affects every part of my being.

If we want to hear our Father's voice, however, we must "tune" our ear to pick up this spiritual communication. Let me explain what I mean. Even as I write this book, the quiet den in which I sit is filled with "sounds." There are literally scores of FM and AM radio signals from across Texas and the Southwest zipping in and through my den— and through my very body—at this instant.

But do you know what? I don't hear a thing.

There are hundreds of television channels and signals, video and audio, literally saturating this "silent" room. And what else? Cellular phone conversations. Two-way and citizen's band and ham radio dialogue. In a sense, this den of mine is vibrating and exploding with sound.

Yet my ears don't pick up any of it. At the moment, it seems perfectly quiet and peaceful. But turn on some appropriate receivers in this room, and hook them to some vibrating speakers, and it could get so loud in here I'd have to run outside to get away from it!

> *God the Father is speaking to us, but we have problems picking up the signal.*

This is true in the spiritual realm as well. We've become poor receivers. God the Father is speaking to us, but we have problems picking up the signal. The communication problem isn't on *His* end, it's on ours. We can't distinguish the voice of our Father from the noises around us. We're distracted. Our hearts are weighed down with anxiety, or hardened by spiritual neglect and sin. We've forgotten how to hear the voice of the Father as He speaks to us.

Our enemy the devil speaks, too, and we must be on guard against those things he would whisper into our ears. A master of disguise, he can come to us like "an angel of light" or as a wolf in sheep's clothing. The key to distinguishing between God's voice and the voice of the enemy is to possess a knowledge of His Word, the Bible, and to study God's character as revealed in the Word and in the life of Jesus.

DULL OF HEARING

At fifty-plus years of age, I have a condition referred to as "dull of hearing." I'm not *hard* of hearing; I can hear most things as well as anyone. But I am *dull* of hearing. That means if there's no other sound around I can hear a pin drop. But if there are any competing sounds in the house, I can't understand what a person speaking in a normal voice is saying. And I have to ask my wife, "What did he say?"

Why am I dull of hearing? Because I have preached loudly for years, and that forces pressure against my ear drums and affects my hearing. Also, most of my preaching through the years has been to audiences of 5,000; 10,000; and 15,000 people in huge coliseums with large amplification systems. I'm also a pilot, and pilots' ears typically become dulled by the constant droning of the airplane engines. As a result of these things, I don't hear distinctly the syllables of words spoken around me.

In the same way, some of us don't hear our own heavenly Father clearly. Yet God *wants* to talk to His people! And as already mentioned, in the Gospel of John, Jesus said that His sheep hear His voice and know His voice.[5] Do you?

As sheep of that same Shepherd, we can know His voice, too. We can discern it through all the competing noises. We can distinguish His voice from the voices of Satan and evil spirits. We can experience its comfort and assurance in the midst of life's turmoil and storms.

We're distracted... we've forgotten how to hear the voice of the Father.

Unfortunately, most of us don't, because we haven't tuned our spiritual ears to listen.

How, then, do we accomplish that sort of spiritual fine-tuning?

TUNED BY THE WORD

I'm convinced that the Bible, God's written Word, is the tuning device that can make such hearing possible. The Bible says, "Faith comes from hearing, and hearing by the Word of Christ."[6]

The Word of Christ is all important! The Bible teaches us how to know God, how to discern the spirits, and how to distinguish His voice from the "interference and static" in the spiritual realm.

But it's more than a matter of simply reading the Bible and giving intellectual assent to it. It's more than seeing printed lines on a page or even committing portions of Scripture to memory. It's been said that

Joseph Stalin had memorized large portions of the New Testament in his youth. Yet what did it do for him? He ended up being one of history's greatest fiends and murderers. Stalin might have read the Word and memorized the Word, but he certainly wasn't hearing the voice of God.

And for us, too, it isn't just reading the Word, it is *how* we read. Are we listening for God's personal voice to us as we read? Are our hearts prepared to respond to the prompting of the Holy Spirit? Are we reading with a believing heart and a wide-open willingness to apply those living truths to our daily lives and individual situations—no matter what? Are we ready to step forward as He directs us and put His promises to the test?

Think back a moment to the incident of Peter walking on water. As a good Jew, Peter was probably familiar from childhood with the stories of God's activities and demonstrations of great power in the Old Testament. He'd heard about the Red Sea. He knew about Jericho. He was aware that God had even stopped the sun in the sky in answer to the prayers of Joshua.

Was that what gave Him courage, then, to step out of that fishing boat onto a stormy sea and walk toward Jesus? No, he walked on the water because Jesus looked directly at him and said, "Come to Me." He heard that command and stepped out, heading straight across the waves. He acted on that word and walked where he had never walked before.

Now, you can read about that event and believe its historical accuracy, as I do. But simply reading about it doesn't mean you can stroll across the water of the nearest swimming pool.

If Jesus were standing out there on the water of the pool, and He looked at you, called you by name, and said, "Come here," then you could do it—if you kept your eyes on Him. But just reading a few paragraphs in the Bible won't get you out on the water. It won't hold you up. You've got to hear the voice of God telling you, "Come."

When God speaks to us and says, "This is for you," then we have the capacity to act on that word. The written Word, revealed and communicated to us by the Holy Spirit within us, somehow gets off the page and moves into our hearts. Then we move forward in faith and obedience.

That's the sort of Bible reading that tunes the ear to hear His voice. And the more you are reading and responding to the living Word of God, the more you will hear your Father direct you in specific areas of your life.

Let me give several examples that changed the very course of my life.

"I WANT YOU TO PREACH"

I've already spoken of how God called me to preach. When I was just a teenager, I heard those words in my spirit, *I want you to be an evangelist.*

And when I whispered, "How can I do it? I'm timid," He whispered back, "Where is your faith?"

"Lord," I said, "it's all in You." (You may recall that Paul had a somewhat similar conversation with God on the Damascus road.)

When I said that, it was settled, because He had the ability to teach me how to communicate boldly and to speak to large audiences in His name and in His power.

"THAT'S THE GIRL FOR YOU"

When I was a young man window-shopping for a wife, I didn't have a dad to counsel me as I counseled my son, Randy. I just knew that I was a healthy young male who liked to look at pretty girls. And as I looked for someone to love and who would love me in return, I remember talking to the Lord about several different young ladies.

"God, look! There she is!" I'd say.

And my Father would patiently reply, "No, that's not her."

And knowing how pretty some of these girls were, I'd say, "Are You sure? *Look a little closer, Lord.*" And He would still say, "That's not the one."

And then what did He do? One night in church He pointed out Betty to me, the sweetest, most beautiful girl in all the world.

"There, son," He told me. "That's *her*. That's the girl for you."

And I'm glad I was listening! I just love her so much. And because God is so big in this woman's heart, she's been able to handle all the pain and failure and struggles in her husband's life through the years. We're really one in the truest sense of the word.

God chose for a teenage boy who never had direction in his life. Because I genuinely wanted His choice, longed after His counsel and wisdom, and listened for His voice, God picked a life partner for me. And He did a great job. She's stuck close to me through some ups and downs that would put a Six Flags roller coaster to shame.

MIDCOURSE CORRECTION!

A number of years ago, God told me I was to move from a large crusade ministry into a studio where I would interact with guests in a daily television program. He reminded me that this was often the posture of Jesus as He ministered—seated informally with small groups of interested individuals, while the world listened and looked on.

It was God who lifted our eyes as a ministry team and told us we would be more effective in outreach if we would help others *all over the world*. As a result, we became Life Outreach International, and went from seeing maybe 100,000 decisions for Jesus Christ in a year to well over a million decisions a year, as we poured ourselves into various nations and peoples around the globe.

More recently, God told me that I would be more personally effective if I'd sit down in a chair in the corner of my office and spend more time listening to Him than I would running my legs off going all over the world. And how true His counsel has been!

Having Fun

When I was a little boy, I especially wanted my dad to take me fishing. If you have been reading this book from the beginning, you know this didn't ever happen. But sometimes I would just sit outside and imagine I was fishing. I now tell people everywhere I go that my Father, God, takes me fishing. My Father loves to see me having fun. He's been an Abba and a Daddy to a man who never had one.

He's been an Abba and a Daddy to a man who never had one.

In using such lighthearted illustrations, I am in no way exaggerating the genuineness of the intimacy we can have in our relationship with the Father. As the old hymn says, "He walks with me and He talks with me." *Yes, we can learn to hear His voice and distinguish sounds in the spiritual realm.* God is far more eager to talk to you and me than we are to listen.

Prayer isn't just communicating our desires, questions, and concerns to God. It also is meditating and remaining silent long enough to hear God speak to our heart through His Spirit. We need to learn to be silent, to listen, to meditate and expect to hear God's voice. The more you do this, the more you begin to recognize and discern His "still, small voice." And remember that His voice will always be consistent with His written Word.

When God Speaks in Unusual Ways

Most dreams we will ever experience in our lifetime are insignificant. They're simply the way our Creator designed our unconscious mind to sort through our thoughts, experiences, worries, and desires.

Nevertheless…if we are listening with all our heart for God's voice, I don't believe we can say God *never* speaks through dreams. In both the Old and New Testaments, we see God using the medium of dreams on numerous occasions to communicate warnings and important information to His people.

And on at least one occasion, He used a dream to save my life.

I dreamed I was pulling out of a particular intersection near my home and watched in horror as a speeding car slammed into the side of my car. Suddenly wide awake and sitting up in bed, I felt my heart pounding in my chest. It had seemed so *real*. Over breakfast, I told my wife about it. I said, "I wonder if that could be a warning. I wonder if He was showing me something that could possibly happen." I was concerned enough that I told all my family members to be extra careful as they were driving and approached intersections.

About a week later, I rolled up to an intersection near my home—

God is far more eager to talk to you and me than we are to listen.

a particularly bad spot where fast-moving oncoming traffic is hidden by a curve in the highway. Waiting at the stop sign, I watched for an opportunity to make a left turn. Straining to see what might be coming around the bend, I saw an oncoming utility van signaling its intention to turn onto my road. That was the opening I was looking for. I stomped on the accelerator and shot forward. I must have moved about five feet out into the intersection when that dream popped into my mind, clear as a video clip.

I slammed on the brakes.

As I did, the van turned, and I saw a small compact car right behind it; the car had previously been hidden from my view. It was speeding in excess of sixty miles an hour and missed the front end of my protruding car by a couple of feet. Had I not immediately moved my foot from the accelerator to the brake, it would have hit me broadside, most likely seriously injuring or killing me.

I share that story for one reason—and it's not to move you toward a daily analysis of your dreams. My point here is just this: God wants to communicate with you and me, His children, more than we'll ever know or understand. And I believe that if we are truly listening for His voice, we will hear *more* of His warnings, *more* of His specific directions, and *more* of His wise counsel.

In the Book of Proverbs, Solomon pictured wisdom as someone shouting aloud in the streets—with no one there to listen.

> Wisdom shouts in the streets. She cries out in the public square. She calls out to the crowds along the main street, and to those in front of city hall.... She cries..."How long will you go on being simpleminded?... Come here and listen to me! I'll pour out the spirit of wisdom upon you and make you wise.
>
> "I called you so often, but you didn't come. I reached out to you, but you paid no attention."[7]

Because we neglect to listen for our Father's voice, because we neglect to tune our ears through His Word, we become dull of hearing and miss what He wants to say to us. We miss His "heads up!" warnings. We miss His counsel. We miss His "golden apples" of encouragement and affirmation.

Any good parent would warn his child of danger ahead. For that reason, I listen to God on behalf of my children. As Peter counsels, I try to stay alert, attentive, and sober-minded in my prayers.[8] And when I speak to my child and say "Be careful," it's not out of paranoia or undue parental concern. I live with the sensitivity to God's Spirit that I pray will become even keener as I listen to Him more.

And as surely as a parent would warn a child, God the Father—Father of all fathers—seeks to warn us when He sees something dangerous or destructive in the path ahead of us. But we don't heed His warnings because we can't hear Him. We're dull of hearing. We're distracted by the noise of our busy lives and all the sounds of our busy world.

I promise you, the reader of this book, that God wants to talk to you. He has a voice; He's never lost it. The God who wrote the Book of Books still has a word, a will, and is anxious to open His heart to you, His own child. Give Him the opportunity! Get to know Him. Walk and talk with Him. Jog or run with Him, if you're so inclined. He can always keep up with you, and He never has to catch His breath.

Do you want to hear Him? Do you *long* to hear Him? Are you willing to do whatever it takes in your life to hear His voice? Then you *will* hear Him! He says you will!

> "You will search for me. And when you search for me with all your heart, you will find me! I will let you find me."[9]

There's a loving, attentive Father who has a few golden apples to roll into your life, if you are ready to receive them.

Just be sure to pass them along. Golden apples are in short supply these days.

Chapter Five

A Father Who Leads Me to the Best

It's what we trust in but don't yet see that keeps us going. [1]

PAUL

When I was a boy, I remember looking around for someone to admire.

Whom should I emulate? Whom might I follow? Who could show me a life worth having, a pattern worth tracing?

My father? God forbid! You have already learned that he was an abusive alcoholic who had abandoned my mother and me for years—then later came back into our lives as a violent threat and an enemy. When I thought about my dad, it was like envisioning a big, dark crater in my heart; there was nothing there to draw me, nothing to follow.

Because of my few years in a stable foster home with the Hale family in Pasadena, Texas, I knew that—somewhere out there—there was at least a possibility of stability. I knew that people actually had homes with running water and electric fans and a car in the garage. I knew that there were families who ate dinner together, spoke kindly to one another, and stayed in the same house for more than six months at a time. I had seen that a couple could have a loving relationship.

I looked at the kids in my neighborhood, and most of them were gang members and thugs. As far as I could see, none of them had ever been successful at anything—except getting into trouble. They were failures. Looking back, I can almost be grateful for that. I was surrounded by third-rate toughs and losers. None of the hoodlums I knew were *successful* hoodlums. I never met any big-time gangster types who dressed well and drove hot cars. If I had, they might have influenced me. But as it was, I knew I didn't want to become one of the losers I saw every day, slouching around on street corners, always in trouble. There *had* to be something better than that.

DREAMS OF A STOCK BOY

At the age of eleven, I started getting out of school every day at noon to work in a grocery store. I worked hard, people liked me, and I began enjoying the first successes I'd ever experienced in my life. I started as a sack boy, moved up to stock boy, graduated to produce boy, and then hit the big time as dairy boy. From that lofty position, I could dare to dream of a job assisting the butcher.

Out of the corner of my eye, however, I kept watching the store manager. He was a kind, quiet man who showed up for work shaved and sober every morning and worked hard all day. He had a car. He had a home. He had a wife and family. He had a good, stable life. *Boy,* I thought. *Maybe someday I can be like him. Maybe someday I can manage a grocery store.*

It seemed like the ultimate dream at that time—and probably beyond the reach of a poor boy like me. But the store manager provided one of the only positive examples I'd ever seen, and no one had ever shown me anything else that I might reach for. If I'd had a dad who cared anything at all about my existence, I might have seen clearly enough to set my heart on a higher star.

Who can begin to measure the impact of a father in giving motivation and direction to a son or daughter? Perhaps, like me, you never had a dad to follow or look up to. Or maybe you did have a father, but for one reason or another, he never talked to you about your potential. Maybe he was either unwilling or unable to give you a glimpse into your future or pass along any hope or wisdom about what you might become or accomplish with your life. He never sat with you on the riverbank, or the front porch, and talked to you about a purpose for living. He never walked with you out under the stars and spoke to you about a destiny that reaches into eternity.

A friend of mine had a father like that. He was a good and godly man and a stable provider for the family, but he never seemed to have a positive or encouraging word for his boy. Consequently, my friend grew up feeling awkward and incompetent at just about everything. One day, when still a boy in high school, his dad happened to hear him making a disparaging remark about himself.

"I could never do anything like that," my friend was saying. "I could never accomplish anything like that."

His dad was silent for a moment. Then he turned to my friend and said, "Son, I think you could accomplish just about anything in life you set your mind to accomplish."

I began to understand that He might have a higher goal for my life.

My friend was stunned and deeply moved. Yet later that day, he felt a bitterness rising in the back of his throat. *If that's really true*, he found himself thinking, *then why haven't you ever told me that before? Why did you wait so long, Dad?*

Children, trying to find their way and their place in the world, are incredibly shapable. As imperfect, frequently preoccupied fathers, we forget what kind of life-molding, destiny-changing impact we can have on our children. We forget (or refuse to admit) that just one positive statement—or one caustic, negative remark—dropped into a child's ears at a vulnerable moment can echo in his or her soul *for a lifetime*.

A FATHER WHO WILL GUIDE

After I became a Christian and came to know God as my Father, I began to understand that He might have a higher goal for my life—something even beyond the meat counter at the corner grocery.

I knew I didn't want the kind of poverty I'd grown up with, and I knew I wanted a solid home and family. I also wanted to own a few nice things, never having had anything as a boy.

In my senior year in high school, I took a law class. A lawyer came to speak to our class one day, and deeply impressed me. I thought, *I wonder if I could be like him. I wonder if I could become a lawyer.* As the year progressed, I began to dream it might be possible. To my surprise, I seemed to have a natural ability to debate and argue my points. So much so that my teacher and a number of students in class had told me, "James, you ought to become a lawyer. You've really got a gift. You really know how to drive home your point."

I thought, *Well, that's good. Lawyers are successful. Maybe I could make a success out of my life.* In my mind, I began pointing myself in that direction. I began building a little dream. At that time, I had no idea what my God-given abilities at persuasion might mean for the future. I was thinking of a courtroom and standing in front of a jury. As great as that idea seemed to me, I would soon learn that God had an even greater vision for my life.

The summer after my senior year a spiritual revival swept through the church I'd been attending. What was especially surprising to me was that it had begun with the youth. I watched in amazement as excited young people got up in front of the church to talk about the Lord Jesus and all He meant to them. At that point, I just didn't know what to think about it. I'd seen kids get excited about God before, and I'd also seen that "holy glow" fade pretty rapidly after a few days. Was this one of those times...or was it for real?

Some time later, when a young visiting evangelist came to speak at a series of meetings at our church, the high school group picked me to be the "guest host." The evangelist's name was Daniel Vestal, now the pastor of a very large church in Atlanta.

Being with Daniel was an eye-opening experience for me—and

maybe that's what that youth group had in mind for a skeptical young man named James Robison. Daniel was excited about God and bubbling over with enthusiasm for the Bible. He had memorized huge portions of Scripture which he would quote from the pulpit. But he would also quote them to me. As host, I had to drive Daniel back and forth to his hotel room, take him out to eat, and even introduce him up on the platform. And Daniel (being Daniel) used the time with me to talk about the Lord and challenge me to memorize Scripture.

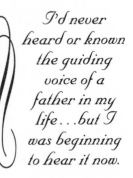

I'd never heard or known the guiding voice of a father in my life...but I was beginning to hear it now.

Something he said must have aroused my competitive nature (which isn't so very hard to do). *Well,* I thought to myself, *if he can memorize like that, I guess I could, too.*

I told my girl friend Betty that I was going to memorize lots of Scripture, and she said that she would, too. So we began working at it together, day after day, night after night. We quoted Scripture to each other when we were in the car and on our dates. And completely unknown to me, my heavenly Father was smiling, knowing what He'd had in mind all along. Our minds and thoughts were being reshaped by the power of His own words.

THE CALL

The One who wrote the Scriptures began to write them in my heart and mind. And as He did, my eyes began to open to His mind and His heart and His will. He began to broaden my field of vision and show me a greater purpose for my life than I could have ever imagined.

This was something new. I'd never heard or known the guiding voice of a father in my life...but I was beginning to hear it now. *Here was a Father who loved me! Here was a Father who had plans and dreams for me!* I can't even tell you how much that realization moved my heart. Then one Friday night, in one of Daniel's meetings, I heard the Father's voice as I had never heard it before. It was clear as a church bell tolling on a frosty morning. It wasn't an audible voice, and yet I could hear it throughout the very fabric of my being.

"James," He said, "I'm calling you to preach. I want you to be an evangelist."

I had been so shy and withdrawn in public—stuttering and stammering through my introductions of Daniel—that when I went forward and announced to the crowd that God had called me to preach, everyone in the building must have thought I'd heard Him wrong. Some even speculated that God must have been calling someone else—and I'd just overheard. I even asked one of the deacons if he thought God could use me to preach. The deacon just smiled at me and shook his head.

It wasn't an audible voice, and yet I could hear it through the very fabric of my being.

"Honestly, son, no. Not to preach."

But I was undaunted. I *knew* God had spoken to me. I *knew* something had happened. God had chosen me for a task, though I had no idea as yet how effective that calling would be if I followed it. I could not have known that He would open the door for me to preach to millions of people throughout North America and all around the world.

Even though my earthly father had seldom spoken to me in anything but a snarl or a curse, I began to understand that my heavenly Father had dreams and plans for me beyond anything I could or would have charted for myself. As I walked out under the stars at night and gazed into His heavens, He was saying to me, "James, I know the plans I have for you.... Plans to prosper you and not to harm you, plans to give you hope and a future. Then you will call upon Me and come and pray to Me, and I will listen to you. You will seek Me and you will find Me when you search for Me with all your heart."[2]

So I heard God at that point leading me to do something I had never really considered. He lifted my head and my vision to a higher goal and purpose than I had ever seen for myself. That's what this Father will do for you as you immerse yourself in His Word and learn to listen for His voice. If you're only seeing your life and your potential through the eyes of an earthly father, if you're only evaluating your abilities and opportunities based on what you've heard from your family or friends, you're selling yourself short. You've limited your scope. Your measure is not what it should be. You are weighing unspeakably important considerations—words about your very destiny—on a scale that may be off by a country mile.

As God once said to one of His servants, "A curse is placed on those who trust other people, who depend on humans for strength, who have stopped trusting the LORD.... But the person who trusts in the LORD will be blessed [or happy]. The LORD will show him that He can be trusted."[3]

When you think about it, who knows your potential better than your own Creator? Who knows what's in the basement and back rooms of your heart like your heavenly Father? David once prayed, "LORD, you have examined me and know all about me.... You know my thoughts before I think them.... You know thoroughly everything I do. LORD, even before I say a word, you already know it."[4] Who knows how to bring the best from your life more than the One who bought you out of the slave market with the sacrificial blood of His own Son? Jesus did that for you—and now lives to lead you into an intimate personal relationship with God.

REMOLDING MY MIND

In one of the first passages I absorbed after Daniel Vestal challenged me to start memorizing Scripture, I came across Paul's words to the Christians in Rome. When it began to dawn on me what he was really saying, I felt like I'd grabbed onto a high-power transmission line.

With eyes wide open to the mercies of God, I beg you...as an act of intelligent worship, to give him your bodies, as a living sacrifice, consecrated to him and acceptable by him. Don't let the world around you squeeze you into its own mold, but let God remake you so that your whole attitude of mind is changed. Thus you will prove in practice that the will of God [is] good, acceptable to him and perfect.[5]

And so by giving myself to the Father, by allowing His Word to actually *remold my mind and my thoughts,* I began to see possibilities I had never seen before. The Word renewed my mind. As a result, I could see clearly, I could hear clearly, and I was able to walk with a clear goal in mind. The Scripture goes on to say, "Don't cherish exaggerated ideas of yourself or your importance, but try to have a sane estimate of your capabilities by the light of the faith that God has given to you all."[6]

That's the key. Seeing ourselves, our lives, our futures, through the eyes of faith…looking beyond what others have

Who knows your potential better than your own Creator?

said about us, to hear what the Father has to say about our usefulness or potential. As the apostle Paul once said, "It's what we trust in but don't yet see that keeps us going."[7]

When God called me to be an evangelist that Friday night so many years ago, I could hardly believe what I was hearing. As Daniel called people to come forward for salvation or to rededicate their lives, I actually began to argue with God. *Lord,* I prayed, *You know I can't speak in public! I have trouble even giving a book report. How could I preach?*

His response to me was clear. "James, where is your faith?"

The more I began to walk by faith and not just by sight, the stronger I sensed the Father's guiding hand on my shoulder. His will began to emerge from the fog and take on sharper focus and definition. And even when He began to tell me staggering, incredible things, I'd already prepared my mind to believe and accept them. God had promised me that if I had the faith to trust in Him, He would give me the power and the words and even the opportunities to preach for Him.

While a freshman in college, I remember one night telling my best friend, Billy Foote, what God had been saying to me.

"Billy," I said, "there's something I want to tell you, but before I do, you have to promise me that you won't tell anyone else and that you won't laugh at me."

Billy and I did a lot of kidding around together. But this time, he could tell I was serious. He said, "Of course I won't laugh, James."

"Promise?"

"Of course. What is it?"

I told him what God had told me—that within a year I would be preaching in the largest churches in America, that I would speak to crowded stadiums and coliseums, and that thousands would stream forward to receive Christ.

Even as I told him about it, the prospect seemed improbable. Crazy. "Wild." What would Billy—who knew me so well—think about what I was saying?

"Billy," I said, "do you think I'm crazy?" I didn't know how he would react. He'd never even heard me speak in public, let alone to huge crowds. I wouldn't have been surprised if he'd just waved off my words or punched me on the shoulder and called me foolish. But he didn't do that. Instead, he walked over to me, put his hand on my shoulder, and looked me straight in the eyes.

"James," he said, "I don't think you're crazy. But I do think we should get down on our knees and pray that you'll never get in God's way."

Is it possible that you could be getting in your Father's way as He reveals His will to you? Are you limiting what He might have in mind for you in the coming days—through apathy or unbelief? Are you taking time to hear the voice of the One who made you and loved you and redeemed your life for Himself? How long has it been since you took a walk under the stars with your heavenly Father, felt His guiding hand on your shoulder, and heard His still, small voice speaking truth in your heart?

And God did do exactly what He said. The doors and opportunities for me to speak literally blew open—over one thousand invitations in a year from across America. Within two years the largest churches, coliseums, and stadiums were filled and overflowing as people came to hear a young man share what seemed to be the very heart of God the Father.

How does it work? How do you open the Bible and find His specific will for your life? In my life, as I discipline myself to read and explore and reflect on God's written Word, I begin to hear Him speak to me about various specific situations in my life. He makes impressions on my heart and on my will, showing me which way to go. The Lord once told His people, "Whether you turn to the right or to the left, your ears will hear a voice behind you, saying, 'This is the way; walk in it.'"[8]

The specifics of His will come as we wait on Him and walk in obedience.

There is nowhere in the Bible where God says, "I want James Robison to be an evangelist." But Scripture does say we are all to be His witnesses—and that he who wins souls is wise. In the same way, there is no place in the Bible where it specifically says, "I want James Robison to marry Betty Freeman." But it does tell me that a good wife is better than earthly riches, and that a man who finds such a wife is blessed by the Lord. And it goes on to tell me what kind of godly qualities to look for in a wife and life partner. The very qualities I found in Betty.

The *specifics* of His will come as we wait on Him, walk in obedience to what we know to be true in His Word, hunger after our Father's best, and seek His face with all our heart.

I'm a pilot and I've always loved to fly at night. Up at ten thousand feet over a darkened landscape, every little light draws your eyes like a magnet. Before you ever draw close to a city, you can look out across the dark horizon and see the beginnings of a distant glow. The closer you fly to the metropolitan area, the brighter that glow becomes, gradually rolling back the darkness. Drawing nearer, you begin to see clusters of bright lights, and even the shapes of buildings. As you fly directly over-head, you can actually see distinct lights from cars on the highway, boats on the rivers, porch lights on back porches, and even the yellow glow of individual windows.

That's the way it often is with the will of God. At first, it seems like a dim light somewhere off on the horizon. Yet there's something about it that keeps drawing you closer—even through darkness and confu-sion and pain. Then, as you continue to press on, as you continue to meditate on your Father's Word and obey your Father's voice, it becomes brighter and brighter...until it finally becomes distinct and clear.

As Solomon wrote, "The path of the righteous is like the first gleam of dawn, shining ever brighter till the full light of day."[9]

Young Solomon might have learned that from his father, David, an imperfect man and an imperfect dad who still had a heart for God. More likely, he learned it from his heavenly Father, who had plans for Solomon beyond the dreams of any earthly dad.

He has plans for you, too. And the earnest pursuit of your Father's will leads to the greatest possible adventure and discovery in your life.

Trust me on that one. Better still, trust Him!

Chapter Six

A Father Who Approves and Accepts

"Fear not, for I have redeemed you;
I have called you by name;
You are mine."[1]

THE LORD, TO HIS PEOPLE

Could a man who has lived every day of his life under an overcast sky find himself missing the warmth of the sun on his face? Could he find himself longing for a blue sky he has never seen?

I really don't know the answers to those questions. (You'll have to ask my friends out in Oregon or Vancouver.)

But here's something else to consider. Is it possible to miss the acceptance and approval of a father when you've never experienced those things? Is it possible to miss something so basic as that when you've never lived with it, when it has never touched your living memory? Yes, I believe it is possible, because I believe that is a longing built into us by our Creator. It's the way He has put us together as men and women. It's part of our internal hard-wiring that never changes. We may not know exactly what it is we are lacking or be able to put words to that gaping hole we feel at the center of our lives, but somehow, we know something isn't right. We know something's missing. We know that life ought to be different.

We also know that deep inside every person there is the desire for others' approval. All children wish to have parents, guardians, family members, or others recognize their achievements when they perform.

81

"*Watch me! Watch this!*" they will plead. How sad when the approval seldom if ever comes. Everyone desires it.

I was reminded of this recently when I came across Paul's words to a group of first-century Christians in Greece. He was reminding them of his last visit and some of the things they had shared together, when he made this comment: "With each of you we were like a father with his child, holding your hand, whispering encouragement, showing you step by step how to live well before God, who has called us into his own kingdom, into this delightful life."[2]

Paul was saying, "I was like a father to you folks during those days...and this is what a father is all about. This is what a daddy does, and how he relates to his sons and daughters. He whispers words of encouragement. He holds his child's hand and gives an extra squeeze that says, 'I'm with you! I like you! I'm proud of you!' He urges his boy or his girl to climb over obstacles, endure failures, persevere through the dry times, find courage in the moments of fear, and reach for the highest and best."

I felt deeply insecure as a boy. I carried a sense of rejection into everything I attempted.

I can't remember experiencing anything like that in my young life. I'm sure I must have tasted it with the Hale family, during those years as a little foster boy in their home. I may have glimpsed it in the lives of others as I grew up, watching fathers relate to their boys and girls on a playground or in a store or at church. But when I searched my own memories and experience for any kind of approval or acceptance, I could find nothing to hang onto. There was no rope to grab hold of down in that dark, lonely pit in which I sometimes found myself.

As a result of that void, I felt deeply insecure as a boy. I lacked confidence and carried a sense of rejection with me into everything I attempted. I think many men can identify with such feelings. Just recently a man told me about his struggles with anger and depression as a young husband. On Saturdays, when he would attempt to do a few simple handyman chores around the house, everything seemed to go wrong.

The jobs may have been "simple," but this man had never been taught by his dad to work with tools. As a boy, whenever he had tried to help with any fix-it jobs, his father would become impatient and seize the tool from his hands, saying, "Here, let me do that." As a result, whenever anything went wrong in his own home, this young man would explode with anger and quickly lapse into melancholy, feeling he "could never do anything right." He remembered one particularly bad Saturday when he became so frustrated with his inability to repair a picture frame, that he hurled his hammer across the family room.

I haven't thrown many hammers in my life, but as a boy, I did like to throw a baseball. Yet even though I was blessed with natural athletic ability, I had trouble making anybody's team. Why? Because my mother and I were constantly drifting from place to place, I was always "the new kid" nobody wanted to choose. Time and again I'd end up being chosen dead last—or not chosen at all.

After a while, I finally caught on to the idea that *if you bring the ball to the game, somebody has to pick you*—whether they want to or not! So I would always try to bring the best, newest ball—even if I had to borrow it from someone.

I remember walking alone down to the city park for Little League tryouts one day, so terrified I felt like I was trying to *swallow* a baseball. Yet when my turn came up, I somehow managed to hit every ball that came across the plate, catch every fly that looped my way, and throw the ball as hard and as straight as any boy there.

Later that afternoon, after everyone had shown his stuff, all the boys gathered in an excited, chattering group while the coaches began to "bid" on players and choose their teams. It was supposed to be fun and exciting, but suddenly all the memories of never being picked and being left out washed across me in a cold wave. *What if no one picks me? What if they leave me standing here alone?*

In the end, I couldn't stand it. I left in the middle of the bidding and walked away from the field, crying all the way home. I needed a daddy on that day. I needed a father to put his hand on my shoulder and say, "Don't worry, son, you'll make the team. You played well and someone's going to pick you for sure. And even if no one picks you, Buddy, I'll *always* pick you."

That's what I needed and longed for. Yet what filled my mind instead was the harsh, condemning face of my father—ridiculing me, cursing me, cursing my mother, making us feel like less than dirt. As a result, I craved approval like most kids crave Hershey bars. I *lived* for moments when someone might tell me I'd done something well, that I could accomplish something or contribute something, or that I had some value as a person.

> *I craved approval. . . . I lived for moments when someone might tell me I'd done something well.*

When I was in high school athletics, the kind of coach that got the best out of James Robison was the one who knew how to praise. The yelling coaches didn't phase me much; I knew all about being yelled and screamed at, and I'd had more profanity flung in my face than most coaches had in their vocabularies. That sort of "motivation" didn't move me at all. But I would put out a hundred and ten percent for the coach who'd drop a word of praise or approval in my direction. I'd lay my body on the line for a coach who'd clap me on the shoulder and say, "Nice play, Robison. Way to be in there, boy."

"PLEASE HOLD ME"

After over thirty years in ministry, I've become convinced that girls and women feel the lack of a father's approval and acceptance every bit as keenly as boys and men do. Sometimes a girl just longs to be held by her daddy. She wants the comfort of his lap, his voice, his arms, his smile, his approval.

I can close my eyes right now and visualize a little scene from a few days ago. I can see my little six-month-old granddaughter resting securely in her daddy's arms. She had her eyes wide open, but seemed *totally* at peace, just snuggled up against his chest, her head with its crown of wispy blond hair resting on his shoulder. My wife Betty went running for the camera, but I just sat there thinking to myself, *Keep it up, son-in-law! Never stop. Don't stop loving her and holding her and saying soft things to her as she begins to grow up! Love that little lady, be there for her, and you'll have a daughter with security and confidence in her heart. You'll have a daughter who'll be able to face whatever life throws at her.*

"Big girls" want physical reassurance, too. At certain times Betty will say to me, "James, would you please hold me?" It's as though she is saying, "No words could comfort me right now. I need arms. I need you to hold me close to your heart for a while."

Many girls have found themselves physically and sexually involved with young men for one reason: Because they are looking for the praise, attention, and affection they longed for from the most important man in their lives, but never received. I've often said that a girl who grows up sitting in Daddy's lap is unlikely to find her way into the back seat of some parked car, or slipping out after dark for a secret rendezvous. There's an inexplicable, confidence-building security that moves in her soul when she rests her head on dad's shoulder and places herself in the arms of a caring father.

Over the years, I've encouraged a number of my friends to take their daughters out on dates. Grant Teaff, football coach at Baylor University and a respected community leader, accepted my challenge and told me he took his daughters out on dates to show them how a boy ought to treat them. Coach Teaff wanted his girls to know what they had a right to expect from young men in their company. *Watch closely, Sweetheart. This is how a gentleman treats a lady.*

How many girls could benefit from this kind of fatherly attention? How many young women might blossom with a steady diet—*from birth*—of their dad's affection, friendship, and approval? How much grief could a girl be spared if her father were to take time to explain the real meaning of modesty, and what it is that stimulates young men and pours gasoline on those ever-smoldering hormone-generated fires? It is what Paul said dads ought to routinely do: *Hold their hand. Whisper encouragement. Show them step by step how to live well, how to walk with God, and how to find a delightful life.*

Sometimes men will speak of wholesome things to their daughters with their mouths while their eyes are telling a very different story.

Girls feel the lack of a father's approval and acceptance every bit as keenly as boys.

Women and girls are extremely conscious of what a man does with his eyes—especially when another woman walks by. Don't ask me to explain it; it's just one of life's mysteries. It's like some kind of sixth sense. And when a dad shows himself again and again to be attracted to seductive and immodestly clad women, whether on television or in a mall, it sends a message to the daughter. *Oh, this is what a man like Dad notices. This is what pleases a man and gets his attention.* So while you may say one thing with your worthy words, your eyes and your actions may send another message entirely—and one you most likely would *not* want to communicate.

I think most girls like to see that spark of approval in their father's eyes and to hear the words, "You look pretty," or "Your hair looks nice," or "I like being with you." When they never hear those things at home, they wonder about themselves. *Am I worthwhile? Am I attractive? Am I likable?* And then there is a tendency to go out and try to attract that kind of attention outside the home, even at the cost of adopting destructive ways.

Through his companionship, attitudes, and warm approval, a father has the opportunity to instill and call forth deep qualities and strengths in his daughter. Through him, she learns how to properly relate to the male sex. And as she watches how her dad treats her mother, she learns the kind of attitudes and treatment she should look for in a potential mate. I often advised girls to watch how boys respond to and treat their own mothers to get a picture of future actions.

This longing for attention and approval common to so many women has been a heartache and a danger to me throughout much of my ministry. When I was in youth ministry, trying to show care and compassion for kids, the girls sensed that I really cared about them. As a result, some of them would turn to me in their distress, looking for comfort and strength and counsel. It put me in highly precarious situations, situations that could have very easily slid into something destructive. It has only been by the great keeping power of God's Spirit that I have been spared from shipwrecking my whole ministry early on.

Why was it such a problem? In many cases, it was because these girls didn't have the approval and positive attention from their dads, leaving them with a deep and unwholesome *craving* for male attention.

Yet in the face of all this, I can say with full assurance that even if a woman or girl never knew or experienced the approval and affection of a daddy, she can find what her heart desires in the heavenly Father. We men, after all, are weak, fallen creatures (in our flesh), and even the best of us can't hope to meet all the needs of a woman's heart. If a woman is hoping and expecting to have all of her thirsts quenched and needs satisfied by a man—*any* man—she is doomed to disappointment. Only a relationship with God the Father can fill a woman's deepest heart needs. Only He can fill up all the lonely places. Only He can bind up the deepest wounds. Only He can give a woman strength to endure the weaknesses, shortcomings, and failures of the men in her life, including her father and her husband.

In so many ways over the years, I have failed as a husband to measure up to the manly character God desires in my life. Yet because my wife understands her heavenly Father's character—and the character of Jesus Christ—she knows how to pray for me. She knows just what kind of strengths and qualities I need to develop to be a godly husband and father, and she holds me up before God every day in prayer. When I make progress, she thanks the Lord. When I fail and fall short, she clings to the Father all the more tightly, to meet her needs and mine. He will *never* fail!

TRYING (SO HARD) TO PLEASE DAD

My friend Larry is a well-known pastor and Bible teacher who almost wrecked his life and ministry trying to gain his father's approval.

His father, now deceased, was a wealthy, successful lawyer who tried to motivate his son through sarcasm and criticism. By actions, expressions, and even words, he told Larry over and over again, "You'll never amount to anything. You're just stupid." When as a young man Larry became a Christian, his parents thought he'd really cashed in his sanity. They even had him checked into a psychiatric ward for analysis.

Yes, he was now off drugs, seemed happier than ever before, and had cleaned up his life...but in their view, this new condition was worse than the first! It was bad enough when their son had a drug problem and dropped out of college. But now he was talking to God? *And God was talking back?* The kid obviously was spaced out on something.

After Larry completed seminary and became a pastor, he enjoyed unusual and remarkable success in ministry—almost from the beginning. In a very short time, he was on his way to becoming a notable, nationally recognized preacher, teacher, and author. But nothing he was ever able to accomplish convinced his father that he was anything more than a "religious nut," and a sorry failure.

In his heart, Larry knew that his dad was judging him by a faulty standard: the standard of material success. Yet even though he knew that, he felt a consuming need to show his dad he could be "successful" in those terms, even if it meant spending lavish sums of money on cars, wardrobe, country clubs, a big house, and all the accouterments of success.

Now, Larry had *already* been successful—in the truest sense. But in a desperate bid to gain his father's acceptance and approval, he ended up damaging and scarring his effectiveness as a Christian leader through overindulgence and materialism. It was all so sad and unnecessary. God the Father, who misses *nothing*, already knew what Larry had been able to accomplish. And more than that, God knew Larry's true identity as a son of the King, with an inheritance in heaven. But the disapproval of his dad so troubled him that he lost sight of eternal realities for a time.

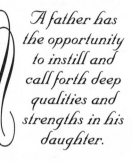

A father has the opportunity to instill and call forth deep qualities and strengths in his daughter.

Larry didn't really need to please an earthly father who possessed a false set of scales. Even so, he and many a man has been haunted by the ghost of a father who withheld acceptance and approval. Many men have become workaholics, wrecked their families, and ruined their health trying so hard to "prove something" to dads who were years in the grave!

"THIS IS WHO I AM"

My friend Milton Green was a wonderful lay Bible student, and the man who helped me through a dramatic deliverance in the early 1980s. The story of his own conversion was gripping, and to hear him tell it would hold people spellbound. But what he loved to do when he got up in front of a group was to simply tell people who he was in the eyes of the Father.

"Do you want to know who I am?" he'd say. "I don't even need an introduction. Let me tell you…" And then, personalizing various portions of God's Word, he would say things like this:

"I've been blessed with every spiritual blessing in the heavenly realms because I belong to Christ. Long ago, before He made the world, God loved me and chose me in Christ to be holy and without fault in His eyes. His unchanging plan has been to adopt me into His own family by bringing me to Himself through Jesus.... He raised me from the dead and seated me with Christ in the heavenly realms.... Throughout eternity God can always point to me, ol' Milt Green, as an example of the incredible wealth of his favor and kindness toward me...."[3] And on he'd go.

Back in the first century, an old fisherman named Peter reminded a group of anxious, beat-up, impoverished Christians to hold their heads high. Even if they were hated and falsely accused by their fellow citizens and hounded by the Roman authorities, they had the approval and acceptance of their heavenly Father and the King of Kings.

Only God can fill up all the lonely places. Only He can bind up the deepest wounds.

"You are the ones chosen by God," he told them, "chosen for the high calling of priestly work, chosen to be a holy people, God's instruments to do his work and speak out for him, to tell others of the night-and-day difference he made for you—from nothing to something, from rejected to accepted."[4]

If we would begin confessing who we really are, who our Father says we are, we would not be so troubled when the devil tries to cut the ground out from under us with his lies. And when our enemy tries to replay the old tapes that say, "You're nothing...You're no good...You're ugly...You're clumsy...You'll never amount to anything...," we need to let the voice of our Father drown them out.

You're mine. You're washed clean. You're important to Me. You're precious to Me. You were worth a Son to Me. You have strength for every situation in My power. You're My son and My delight. You're My very own daughter. You're a child of the King. You're a fellow servant with the mighty angels of heaven. You have an inheritance in My house that's beyond your understanding.

Now as I experience growth and development in my own life, I truly sense God making impressions on my mind: "That's good, James. You're doing well, son. Way to go!" I believe I hear God telling me He is pleased with me.

I remember the time when my sweet wife, Betty, was lying beside me in bed, weeping. We had just been to a wonderful meeting with great spiritual impact. There in the quiet darkness, she said, "I just feel like God's holding me in His arms. He's telling me He's pleased with me! He knows I truly love Him, and He's telling me how much He loves me."

It was one of life's precious moments. Every girl, woman, boy, and man needs to experience that deep sense of God's approval. Our hearts cry out for approval, and God our Father is so anxious to give it.

It still hurts to remember how my father cursed me and thought so little of me. It still hurts to remember the days when I needed to hear even one encouraging word, but never heard it. Yet since I gave my life to Christ as a teenager, I've had a heavenly Father who has told the truth about me—truth that has sustained me through trials, through accusations, through incredible pressures, and through long, dark valleys.

He's your Father, too. And He has truth to tell you, no matter what you have heard in your past, no matter how many lies have been thrown at you and ground into you through the years. Here's a Dad who will tell you the truth. And the truth is, He loves you and values you and has plans for you that can't even be expressed in our poor language.

David was so overwhelmed by these thoughts that he told the Lord,

You saw me before I was born. Every day of my life was recorded in your book. Every moment was laid out before a single day had passed. How precious are your thoughts about me, O God! They are innumerable! I can't even count them; they outnumber the grains of sand! And when I wake up in the morning you are still with me![5]

MY FATHER'S APPROVAL

As I said, I know what it means not to be chosen. I know what it means to be left standing in the field after the teams have been picked. As a boy, I had all the adversity and disadvantages and potential for vice and crime that a boy could know. But when I finally looked up into my heavenly Father's face and accepted His grace and kindness in Jesus Christ, I found the approval and acceptance I'd always longed for.

I'm here to testify that every missing piece in your heart, every unhealed wound, every adversity you've had to endure, can find healing, reconciliation, and completeness as you come to know the Father God as your personal Father.

Chapter Seven

A Father Who Corrects

*"The one whom God corrects is happy,
so do not hate being corrected by the Almighty."*[1]

THE BOOK OF JOB

I was walking through the grocery store, picking up a few items, when it happened—right in front of my eyes. It was horrible. The screams still linger in my memory.

Was it a mugging? An armed robbery? A brutal murder in the cereal aisle?

No, but something almost as chilling. I'm referring to an out-of-control three-year-old on the rampage. *Screaming* defiance at a bewildered mother, he began pulling every item within reach off the shelves and tossing them onto the floor.

His mother stood there watching, wringing her hands, biting her lower lip. "Darrin," she said, "don't do that." It sounded more like a plea than a command, and the little terror completely ignored her. The look on Darrin's face clearly said, *Just watch me.*

He not only continued emptying the shelves, he began throwing some of the items in his mother's direction. The only words spoken with any kind of authority in that aisle came from the lips of Darrin himself, who shouted "No! No! NO!" as he wreaked havoc on one aisle, then ran to another while his mother trailed anxiously behind.

When she finally caught up to him and took hold of his arm, Darrin jerked out of her grasp, stuck his tongue out at his mother, and screamed in her face, *"Leave me A-LONE!"*

Yes, I thought to myself, *that's the problem right there. His parents have left him alone. They've let the boy grow up without any concept of discipline, boundaries, or limits. And they're already paying the price.* It was a clear demonstration of what happens when self-centered or child-centered parenting is practiced in place of God-centered training.

I felt certain that day that if I could have met the father in the family (if there was a father in the family), I would have seen a major contributing factor to the child's behavior. The situation had "missing dad" or "passive dad" written all over it.

I felt sorry for that mom. Without being a prophet, I knew her future didn't look good. If she had so completely lost all control of her child at age three, what was she going to do when he was fourteen and looking down at her with anger burning in his eyes? What then?

Most of all, I felt sorry for the little boy. Unless something changed in his life very soon, he was headed for a bitterly unhappy life at best, and possibly toward personal destruction at an early age.

Solomon wrote: "Correction and discipline are good for children. If a child has his own way, he will make his mother ashamed of him."[2] Still more ominous, however, is Solomon's prediction of what happens when a child who has never learned discipline grows up:

"An evil man is held captive by his own sins; they are ropes that catch and hold him. He will die for lack of self-control; he will be lost because of his incredible folly."[3]

Those frightening words could have easily been the James Robison story.

WHERE ARE THE LINES?

Growing up as I did without a dad to guide or discipline me, I might readily have made choices as a teen that would have tied me up as with ropes, my lack of self-control holding me captive. I'd be willing to bet that a number of the boys I ran with as a teen are now doing time in a penitentiary somewhere—or have died violent deaths. In fact, I know this is true of some.

Without a father's correction in my life, I did lack discipline. And while the Lord spared me from getting myself killed or into serious trouble, there were so many secrets of life and points of wisdom I wished I had learned early on, but did not. I didn't understand self-control. I didn't have a grip on self-discipline. Most of the time, I didn't even know how to be courteous or polite. It wasn't that I was deliberately being selfish or rude, I just didn't know any better. No one had shown me how to behave. No one had modeled for me the way a man ought to act or speak or respond. No one had watched my actions and checked me when I got out of line. Half the time, I didn't even know where the lines were!

I might readily have made choices as a teen that would have tied me up as with ropes.

As a result, I endured some deep embarrassment and difficult days when in my late teens I moved in with the Hale family. The more I watched these kind, courteous people respond to one another in disciplined, mannerly ways, the more I became aware of how woefully short I fell of decent behavioral standards. Everyone was patient and gracious with me, but I felt humiliated. I really struggled.

That lack of discipline and training showed up again when I was a young man—in Bible college, and later, in the ministry. I had no idea how to order and prioritize my own time. I didn't know how to study, how to budget, or how to schedule myself. Some of my God-given gifts made me appear sufficiently effective that I "got away with" some old sloppy habits. But sooner or later, lack of discipline will show! And it may show in humiliating ways.

HOMES ON A HILL

All along the way, however (beginning at the home of the Hales), I had the privilege of rubbing up against parents and families who were doing it right. When I read how the Lord Jesus spoke of His followers being like cities on a hill, I think of marvelous Christian couples and families whose homes shine brightly in the growing darkness of our world. And as our culture becomes more and more coarse, crude, careless, and self-centered, I recall the graciousness, poise, manners, and joyful expressions of the parents and children in those godly families. No, these families are not perfect or trouble free; a certain amount of heartache is part of the tuition for living in a broken world. And yet these homes stand in such stark contrast to the homes and families around them that they cannot help but attract attention.

I think that's what the apostle Paul had in mind when he wrote to his friends in Philippi: "Do everything without complaining or arguing, so that you may become blameless and pure, children of God without fault in a crooked and depraved generation, in which you shine like stars in the universe as you hold out the word of life."[4]

Our family wasn't perfect, either. Not by a long shot. But by God's grace, Betty and I learned together through the years about making positive contributions in the lives of our children through correction. We learned what it means to *train* a child, not just "tell" them. There really is a difference. You can tell a child something over and over, but if you do not enforce your requests or your commands, if you don't diligently follow through with consequences clearly promised and promptly delivered, then you're actually training that boy or girl to respond in a negative fashion. All of the right teaching in the world won't shape a child's life unless you train him or her to properly *respond* to that teaching.

> *Sooner or later, lack of discipline will show! And it may show in humiliating ways.*

A child is neither a horse nor a dog, but there are a few things we might consider here when we mention the word "training." A good horse in the arena is trained, not simply taught. A number of years ago, I watched a world champion show horse stepping through its paces in an arena. I was amazed at how quickly the horse responded to the lightest touch of the reins or the slightest pressure of the rider's leg on its neck or flank. The horse was trained to respond, and did so to perfection.

I've observed beautiful bird dogs working in the field, and been awed by their instant response to their owner's voice. Against all natural inclination, they are trained to hold perfectly still when they locate birds in the field. Instinct might lead these dogs to find a covey of quail, but it is only training that keeps them from prematurely rushing in and flushing the birds. These animals are not just taught or told, they are trained—until their responses become almost automatic.

Admittedly, you can carry this comparison just so far. But I use it to make a point. Parenting involves far more than simply explaining matters to our children (and then supposing our job is done).

Our culture today puts great stock in the notion that our children "need more education" about harmful things like drugs, alcohol, or illicit sexual activity. Over and over again, we're told that the answer to the drug problem or teenage pregnancy or sexually transmitted disease is "more education" in our schools. There seems to be this unyielding belief that if we use class time to pour more and more *information* on a problem, it will somehow resolve itself and go away. As if a quantity of proper data is all that a child lacks to be perfectly behaved.

Not so!

It isn't more information or statistics on teenage drinking and carousing that will turn these problems around.

It isn't more brochures, pamphlets, condom distribution, or graphic sex education in the early grades that will bring down the illegitimate birthrate or decrease the number of abortions.

It isn't more education in the schools that we need, it's more *training* in the home. What is needed are alert, involved mothers and fathers setting Bible-based standards of behavior, living out those standards by example, and then backing those standards with consistent, loving correction.

"I'VE TOLD YOU AND TOLD YOU..."

You've seen it happen, just as I have. In a normal tone of voice, a parent tells a child not to do something. The child pauses, thinks a moment, and then goes ahead with the deed anyway. The parent then raises the decibel level and shouts at the child. The child may look up in bewilderment, but all the while he will be closely watching his parent's actions. You can almost read the question on his face: *What happens if I don't?* The child persists in the activity and the parent screams again—louder this time. But there is still no correction taking place. What *is* taking place, however, is the breaking of fellowship between parent and child. Resentment, anger, and defiance build between them, and they become more and more estranged from one another.

Do you see how that works? If as a parent you give a command, see that it has no effect, and then begin counting "ONE...TWO... THREE..." or maybe "ONE...TWO...TWO-AND-A-HALF...TWO-AND-THREE-QUARTERS..." you are actually training the child *not* to obey your initial command, but rather to respond only to your threats or your timed counts. If you are a shouter, you train the child only to respond when you shout. The kids come to understand that "Dad is now screaming and turning red in the face, so now I know he really *means* it."

This is what I mean by training. You can tell your kids something. You can explain why you're telling them and why it's best for them to do certain things. You can teach them, and you may still find the child going his or her own way. What do you do? *You reinforce your words with firm, loving, appropriate correction.*

It would be nice, of course, if you knew all of these things before your first child came along. Most of us, however, learn some of our parenting lessons through painful courses in the School of Experience. And firstborn children get to go to that school with us!

Rhonda, our first child, turned out just fine, thank the Lord. But looking back, we can't help but wish we had understood some of the skills we later developed with our second and third children, Randy and Robin. Life would have been so much easier and less stressful, for Rhonda and for us.

THE ROD OF CORRECTION

Here is what we learned that worked so effectively for us. We would tell our children to do something in a normal tone of voice. If they didn't respond or do what we told them to do, we would *immediately* correct them. At different ages, various means of discipline were effective. Older children might be sent to their room, denied a privilege, or not allowed to participate in certain activities or be with favorite friends.

When they were small children, we found that the biblical reference to a training rod worked very effectively. We found it best to refrain from spanking a child with our hand, knowing they would begin associating our hands with punishment. When discipline *was* administered directly by a parent's hand, it seemed that rather than fearing the consequences of their actions, our children actually feared the actions of the parent. The same would be true of a belt, taken from the parent's person.

Reinforce your words with firm, loving, appropriate correction.

To our amazement, however, we discovered the incredible accuracy of biblical truth by using a "rod," which in our case was a small, flexible switch. The flick of a switch applied to the hand or leg of a child simply stings. There is no call or need to strike or bruise a child, or inflict severe pain. That is not correction, it is abuse.

We were amazed how quickly our little ones responded to the rod of correction. Employing that little switch was neither unkind nor abusive. It was, on the contrary, one of the kindest things that could have happened to our children.

When the child disobeys, he or she needs—ever so desperately—to understand that the consequences of rebellious actions bring about painful experiences. It is one of the greatest, most important lessons in all of life. The pain a parent inflicts with a switch is little more than a sting that quickly fades. But if the child does not learn about consequences, the pain that will come about later in life will be deep, crushing, and unbelievably severe.

So which is best? A little minor pain now…or untold life-shattering pain later in life?

The Bible itself insists that such discipline works. Just listen…

He who spares the rod hates his son, but he who loves him is careful to discipline him…. Discipline your son, for in that there is hope; do not be a willing party to his death…. Folly is bound up in the heart of a child, but the rod of discipline will drive it far from him…. Do not withhold discipline from a child;…punish him with the rod and save his soul from death…. Discipline your son, and he will give you peace; he will bring delight to your soul.[5]

Despite the time-tested biblical guidelines established long ago, many people today choose to discard Bible truths, settling instead for the opinions of sociologists, psychologists, newsstand magazines, radio talk-show hosts, or even next-door neighbors.

Betty and I chose to apply the biblical principles of discipline when the children were very young. As a result, we did not have to resort to shouting, nagging, bribing, or threatening. We just said, "Don't do that," and they would stop, knowing what would happen *immediately* if they didn't. By the time our children reached the age of five, I don't recall more than a few times over the course of their growing-up years when the need of serious discipline became an issue.

THE FATHER'S CORRECTION

In this light, I think it is so important to understand that God, our wonderful Father, loves us enough to bring correction into our lives. As a matter of fact, He says clearly in Scripture that if we're without discipline in our lives, we're not even legitimate children. We're not truly spiritually born as children of God.[6] He corrects those He loves.

As the writer to the Hebrews put it:

> Our earthly fathers disciplined us for a few years, doing the best they knew how. But God's discipline is always right and good for us because it means we will share in his holiness. No discipline is enjoyable when it is happening—it is painful! But afterward there will be a quiet harvest of right living for those who are trained in this way.[7]

What, then, is the "rod" or "switch" our heavenly Father uses in our lives to guide us away from danger and into abundant life? Some of the principal means He employs are the natural consequences of our own sins and rebellion. "Don't be misled," He tells us in Scripture. "Remember that you can't ignore God and get away with it. You will always reap what you sow! Those who live only to satisfy their own sinful desires will harvest the consequences of [defeat, pain] and death. But those who live to please the Spirit will harvest everlasting life from the Spirit."[8]

While Jesus paid the ultimate penalty for our sins on the cross, there are inevitable consequences built into our sins that we cannot avoid. King David was forgiven for his sins of adultery and murder, yet the *results* of his actions continued to bring him turmoil and sorrow for the rest of his life. I believe that the consequences of our sins are like a fixed force—a wall that we throw ourselves against, to our own pain and injury. The laws of God are immovable. They are fixed, and they are fixed for our protection, not to imprison us.

God has given us His controlling laws and commandments for our benefit, in much the same way that a parent gives a small child boundaries for his play. "Stay in the backyard. Don't step off the curb." Why? Because it's safe in the backyard. Why not step off the curb and into the street? Because there is danger in the street. The parent is not trying to limit the child's pleasure, but rather extend the potential for joy through the entire life of that precious little one.

Many parents, out of great love for their little ones, will actually fence the backyard and seek to securely lock it. Again, this is not a prison. These are boundaries which are not intended to shackle the child, but to eventually release him to a fuller, wider, happier life.

Let's imagine that a child rebels and determines to escape that secure backyard. If he can't get through the gate, he finds a way to scale the fence. (We can be so ingenious and resourceful in pursuing our own destruction!) The child not only goes over the fence and across the curb, he plays with careless abandon in just the place he wanted to be all along...in the middle of a busy street.

If the child does not learn about consequences, the pain later in life will be severe.

What is likely to happen? An accident! An injury! The child could suffer some minor hurt or perhaps sustain serious, even life-threatening injury. As a matter of fact, the child's life could be snuffed out in an instant—and all his potential erased from the face of this earth.

If we could only see the commands of God as the protective "hedge" spoken of in the Book of Job, how much more joy we would experience and how much deeper our appreciation would be for the love, compassion, and genuine watch-care of our heavenly Father.

When we step over the line, the consequences of our actions close in on us. And it stings! It aches! It brings us frustration and grief! This is the corrective hand of God.

Some people (perhaps because of their experience with a harsh earthly father) seem to picture some growling, angry God standing over His children with a big club. They visualize Him continually looking over their shoulder, so that He might catch them in some indiscretion or sin and lower the boom on them.

The more accurate picture is one of a loving parent, holding out His arms to His wandering children…but willing to use the rod of correction to keep them from greater harm and deeper grief.

Some people I have known imagine God driving up and down the road trying to *run over* those disobedient children who insist on playing in the street. In fact, nothing could be further from the truth. The Book of Proverbs pictures Wisdom and Truth actually standing at the head of every street, calling out a warning to the foolish:

Wisdom calls aloud in the street, she raises her voice in the public squares; at the head of the noisy streets she cries out…"How long will you simple ones love your simple ways? How long will mockers delight in mockery and fools hate knowledge? If you had responded to my rebuke, I would have poured out my heart to you and made my thoughts known to you."[9]

He's calling to us, "Get out of the street! Come back! My little one, come to Me! There is danger! Come back and find safety and healing." And if you stop to consider the implications of what happened on the cross, we have a picture of a God who actually throws Himself in front of the oncoming traffic in order to rescue us and save us from eternal death.

God is constantly seeking to turn us from actions that will bring hurtful consequences into our lives. Wounded and beat up as we are by our rebellious ways, He calls us back to the path of healing. As it says in the Book of Hebrews, "Therefore, strengthen your feeble arms and weak knees. 'Make level paths for your feet,' so that the lame may not be disabled, but rather healed."[10] He's actually trying to give us a way of escape, a way to turn, a way to get back into the safety of a hedged life, a protected life.

He longs to train us. He longs for us to simply heed His Word, so that we will not have to endure the consequences of sin. If we would only listen!

ONE MAN'S EXPERIENCE OF CORRECTION

A number of years ago, when I spent time with Jim Bakker at his PTL ministry, I must admit that I did not have much respect or affection for the man. Nor did I like some things I saw at PTL—even in the early days when that ministry was riding high. I was troubled by what I encountered there. Something seemed seriously amiss. I saw Bible truths twisted and used for gain, and I witnessed compromised lives. It was very disturbing.

In those days, God had newly opened my heart and given me a real love for all parts of the Christian community—including those branches of the family I had previously scorned and even preached against. And though I didn't agree with the actions and priorities of some of these groups, I deeply wanted to try and help them.

As a result, I went to PTL and spoke directly to Jim and Tammy Fae Bakker. I spoke to them in private, and I spoke to them openly and publicly in their meetings and on television. Initially, Jim seemed to listen…but ultimately he shut me out. Consumed as he was by his vision of building a PTL empire, he did not want to listen to a message of caution.

On one of his television programs, I even pointed out what one of the Old Testament prophets said—that you could actually fornicate with wood and stone. I sought to make the point that we can let our dreams and desires to build physical structures lead to fornication with buildings! The Lord told the prophet Hosea that Israel had forgotten her Maker and built temples.[11] It's possible to forsake God and at the same time build ministries and churches in His name! As strongly and publicly as I knew how, I called on the Bakkers and PTL to repent and turn back to Him.

Jim Bakker later expressed in his own book, *I Was Wrong,* that there came a time when he realized I'd been trying and trying to help him. He said that in hindsight, he fervently wishes he had listened to me and others who were warning him. But at that time he just couldn't seem to hear.[12]

The Bible talks about people who become willingly blind; even though they have eyes, they can't see. In the Book of Isaiah, the Lord laments, "Who is blind but my servant?... Who is blind like the one committed to me?... You have seen many things, but have paid no attention."[13] People who turn away from the Lord don't want to see and hear what He has to say to them. And after they have closed their eyes and ears to Him long enough, they become blind in fact. They can no longer see the path before them or hear the voice of God.

That's where Jim Bakker was. But God is a loving Father who knows how to correct His own. Jim Bakker ended up in federal prison. The consequences of his actions brought him down.

But as Jim pointed out to me when I visited him in prison (and has pointed out to me several times since), God in His love put him in a situation where he had no choice but to listen! Jim knows now that it was the discipline of a loving Father that put him in prison. In retrospect, his *forty-five year sentence* was incredibly harsh and unjust. Rapists, murderers, and child abusers don't usually get that kind of sentence! And yet Jim Bakker (now out on parole) says it was the most wonderful thing that ever happened to him.

We did not have to resort to shouting, nagging, bribing, or threatening.

This man is truly transformed. The joy in his heart is *real*—not something manufactured for the television cameras. His children, who had drifted far from the Lord, have become beautiful, radiant Christian adults involved in ministry themselves, and they are raising godly families.

Jim Bakker is now enjoying his children and grandchildren. They're the delight of his life. And he almost missed that joy by being consumed by his religious vision and his own zeal. The hand of the Lord came down hard on this man, but as others have written, it was "a severe mercy."

Jim Bakker couldn't be more grateful for God's discipline and correction. His painful experience was the result of crossing over the line defining God's established boundaries, and a lack of sensitivity to God's will.

Just as the father in the story of the prodigal son, God allows us to turn our backs on Him, go our own way, throw away our privileges as sons and daughters, and even end up in the "pig pen," in great hunger and need. But as with the young man in our Lord's story, the harsh consequences of our actions may very well bring us to our senses. We may say, as that young man said, "I will set out and go back to my father."[14] He got up and walked out of that pig pen of a life and went back to the father—who was waiting for him with forgiveness, provision, and wide open arms!

That's precisely what repentance is. It's not just saying, "I'm sorry." It's not *remorse*, it's not *regret*, it's not *reform*, and it's certainly not *religion*. It is a *return* to the Father with your whole heart.

And the Father God is looking at every person reading this book and saying, "Will you come to Me right now with your whole heart?" No matter how far you've strayed, no matter what you've done, no matter how much you've failed, no matter how deeply you've managed to dig your way into the pit of your own actions and destructive ways, God says, *"I am longing for you to come back into My arms. You have never been out of My heart."*

Chapter Eight

A Father Who Teaches

I was given mercy so that in me, the worst of all sinners,
Christ Jesus could show that he has patience without limit.
His patience with me made me an example
for those who would believe in him and have life forever. [1]

PAUL, TO TIMOTHY

During so much of my childhood and youth, I had no example to follow, no father role model to teach me and show me the way.

As a result, I didn't know how to be an effective teacher for my own children. Impatient perhaps with my own shortcomings, I became overly impatient with theirs. Remembering my own lack of opportunities as a child, I wanted to push, pull, and hurry my children ahead into all of their opportunities. When they failed to live up to my high expectations or weren't as intense as I thought they ought to be, I could be quick to express my anger and displeasure. Without even realizing it, I was becoming sharp and harsh with them.

TEACHING WITH PATIENCE

Over the years, my family came to realize that those sharp little outbursts didn't really portray the deep feelings of my heart; it was just a bad habit I had fallen into. Nevertheless, that sort of harsh, negative dealings with children can inflict real stress—and even lasting damage.

I had a great deal to learn about becoming a patient teacher.

I can recall on more than one occasion trying to get our son's attention, to get him to focus his undivided thoughts and energies on the subject at hand, whether it was a chore at home or a school assignment or an athletic activity. I noticed that when I dealt sharply with him, he would shake himself out of his daydreams and focus his attention more keenly on his task. So (I told myself), it was a "method" that worked.

When my son was about ten years old, I agreed to become the coach of his YMCA Little League football team. It wasn't easy, with my crusade schedule and travels being what they were, yet I had a nagging feeling I needed to be spending more time with my boy. He seemed to be growing up so much faster than I'd imagined he would! My desire was a good one...yet I almost ruined the opportunity with my impatience and high "performance standards."

The boys on the team seemed to like me and responded well to me. But then...everything seems rosier when you are winning, and we were winning! It was an exciting time. The trouble was, I got so caught up with the goal of our becoming a championship team that I forgot we were supposed to be having fun and enjoying one another. As well as we were performing, I just knew those little fellas could do even *better* (particularly my own son, who in my mind had all kinds of untapped potential). In my zeal, I got tough with the boys. I shouted and scolded and criticized, challenging them to push themselves harder and improve their game.

I got so caught up with the goal...I forgot we were supposed to be having fun.

It wasn't a bad strategy, I suppose, if you're a pro football coach. But these weren't salty, hardened veterans; they were little boys. On one occasion in particular I knew in my heart that I'd overdone it. I'll never forget the conversation I had with my son Randy that night at home.

I sat down beside him.

"Buddy," I began, "are you...that is, do you think I might have been, well, a little hard on the boys today?"

He looked up at me and answered gravely, "Perhaps you were, Dad."

Those were his exact words, and it stopped me in my tracks for a moment. The sentence sounded so mature coming from the mouth of a ten-year-old.

"Well," I said, "do you think they understand that I really love them, even though I may talk harshly to them?"

"Yes," he replied, "I think they do."

"Do you think maybe I ought to apologize to them for my sharp tone of voice?"

"I think that might be a good idea, Dad."

That was all that was said about it, but in his gentle way, I knew Randy was honestly telling me that I'd been a little over the line with my criticism and driving impatience. I think it meant a lot to him that I was willing to back off and humble myself with an apology and an admission of guilt.

I remember another occasion when Randy played extremely well in Little League baseball. He had actually batted .500 that year and, as I recall, had only two singles. He was primarily hitting doubles—and also some triples and home runs. He was consistently driving the ball up against the outfield fence on one or two bounces—good enough for extra bases in Little League. He was having the year of his life, and this daddy felt pretty puffed up about it all.

He was doing well in the field, too. I remember the time he caught a long fly ball just at the fence line. It was the third out and we were clapping, stomping, and hollering. All of this excitement wasn't lost on our three-year-old daughter Robin, who had been playing around the bleachers.

"What happened?" she said, scuttling up the bleachers to join us.

"*Randy caught a fly!*" we shouted, joy radiating from our faces.

She considered this, and watched the boys trotting triumphantly back to the dugout. Little Robin ran over to the chain-link fence and peered through at her brother as he joined his happy team on the bench.

"Hey, Bubby!" she yelled. "Let *me* see that fly!"

She thought her brother was out snagging flying insects, and from the way we were reacting, she assumed he must have caught something pretty special.

Yet even with the great year he was having, Randy seemed to be on the bench quite a bit as the coaches tried to play as many boys as possible. Always polite, Randy had a great attitude about it, and seemed content to give others their turn in the spotlight. He wasn't struggling a bit.

But I was!

More than once, I told that coach how I felt about it. How could he pull a kid who was having such a year? How could he replace him with boys who didn't care nearly as much or play nearly as well? Didn't he want to win? Wasn't he sending the wrong signals by benching the kids who were playing the hardest and best?

As a matter of fact, there really were some wrong signals on that field. But they weren't coming from the coach. It was my own impatient, win-at-all-costs attitude that was sending the wrong signals!

Randy didn't like having his dad in the coach's face. It made him nervous and embarrassed him. He would find himself looking over his shoulder, wondering how Dad was going to react to this or that decision. It was something of a shadow right in the midst of that superb year. Down in my heart, I knew that my attitude bothered him—and I asked the Lord to help me back off a little.

TEACHING BY ENCOURAGEMENT

When Randy made the all-star team we were all excited as could be. I can remember flying home from a crusade and getting to one of the all-star games just a little bit late. As I walked up to the ball diamond from the parking lot, I could see that Randy's team was already in the field and my heart started pounding a little bit harder.

But where was Randy? I approached the bleachers and there he was, sitting by himself on the bench. Good night! It didn't make sense! This was the kid who led the league in batting averages and had played so well in the field. And he was starting the all-star game *on the bench?*

Randy looked unsmilingly over his shoulder as he watched me take my seat in the bleachers. Seeing the expression on his face, I honestly felt as though I could read his mind. He was thinking: *Oh, man. I know Dad is really disappointed and upset to see me on the bench. Dear God, please don't let him say anything or let it show.*

By the grace of God, that was one of those moments when I finally got it right. While I was still in my car driving from the airport to the game, I felt strongly impressed that I somehow needed to convey to that young man how thoroughly proud I was of him—and that he didn't need to "perform" to get my approval.

I needed to convey how thoroughly proud I was of him...he didn't need to "perform" to get my approval.

I walked over to the fence and leaned over. My boy looked up, somewhat apprehensively.

"Randy," I said, "I want you to know Dad is just as proud of you sitting right here on this bench as I would be if you were starting at third base and hitting home runs. There's no way I could ever be more proud of you. You're my son, and you don't have to do anything to please me or to gain my approval. You've got it a hundred percent. I love you, son."

Tears filled his eyes and he smiled. Somehow I knew I had touched a chord. And with thanks in my heart to God, I knew I had done exactly the right thing.

TEACHING BY OUR FAILURES

From that time on, that was the message I tried to communicate to my son—and my daughters, too—over and over. I wanted them to understand right down to their bones how completely pleased we were with them. I wanted them to know that anytime we challenged them or tried to point out a better way to approach something, we were doing it with their best interests at heart.

Many people I've known make the mistake of communicating the idea that "family reputation" is more important to them than their children's feelings or concerns. This is especially true in many church-going families. Dad and mom seem inordinately worried about damaging some kind of an "image" in front of the church body or the community.

When children realize that the family's so-called "image" is more important than their needs and feelings, they can feel hurt or resentful. I personally think we should be willing to blow that precious image to smithereens for the sake of the well-being of those we love. *Who cares what so-and-so in the church thinks! Who cares what the neighbors or Aunt Harriet thinks!* Others' opinions don't even weigh in the balance with the needs and feelings of our children.

Our positive example can grow in value for years to come. The dividends are great.

One of the more meaningful things Betty and I did with our children was to readily acknowledge and admit to our own weaknesses and failures. When we made mistakes or exercised poor judgment, we approached our children and asked for their forgiveness. When as a couple we had hurt or offended one another, we asked each other's forgiveness in the presence of our children. We wanted them to see us humbling ourselves before one another.

I think some of the most special moments I ever had with my children were in those dark hours when I had to sit down and tell them, "Kids, your daddy has messed up. I've blown it big time, and I want you to know that." There's no way to describe the comfort that comes from having your own children come and say, "Dad, we know it hurts and we hurt with you. It hurts us all, because we're a team—just like you've always told us. But we love you, Daddy."

Facing the issues of our own frailty in such a way enables our children to face their own failures with perspective and courage. They come to understand that a failure—even a big one—isn't the end of the world.

Beyond what we may ever say to our children, however, the greatest teaching tool we have is the example of our own lives. Those who have ignored this principle have learned to regret it very deeply.

TEACHING BY EXAMPLE

A number of years ago, I heard a true story I've never forgotten. A Christian dad, it seems, had come to some rather firm convictions about alcohol. He made it very clear that he believed moderate drinking was perfectly acceptable for believers. He knew the Scriptures, and knew that the Bible condemned drunkenness. But there was nothing in the Bible, he maintained, that actually prohibited the moderate enjoyment of alcoholic beverages. This was something of a point of pride with him; he held strong opinions on the subject. He kept a liquor cabinet in his home, and wanted everyone to know he was not in the least ashamed of it.

What he hadn't considered, however, was the effect this rather militant stance might have on his teenage daughter. A high-schooler nearing graduation, this lovely girl had been chosen queen of the prom. Her date, the "king" of the prom, had received a brand-new sports car from his wealthy parents as a graduation present. On prom night, he rolled up in front of his girlfriend's house in that shiny new car and the two of them headed off in all their finery.

The girl's proud father watched them drive away with a lump in his throat. How grown up she had looked. What a beautiful young woman his little girl had become—almost overnight it seemed. He and his wife retired for the night with happy hearts. But they were awakened with a start in the early morning hours by the ringing of the phone.

Shaken but still somewhat groggy, he groped for the receiver. It was the police. "Sir," said a grave voice on the other end of the line, "there's been an accident on the outskirts of town. You need to come to the scene. We think your daughter may have been involved."

Heart pounding in his throat, the man leaped out of bed, threw on some clothes, and sped the short distance to the intersection the officer had told him about. As he approached, he could see the flashing lights of emergency vehicles off in the distance. Police cars. An ambulance. As he pulled up to the scene, he saw firemen...trying to free two people from the mangled wreckage of a small sports car. The little car was barely recognizable. How could anyone have lived through such a crash?

In fact, they hadn't. The father watched in unbelieving horror as the rescue workers pried the car apart and removed the bodies of his precious daughter and her boyfriend. The king and queen of the prom were dead. With a shattered heart, he stared into the wreckage. Taking a few steps closer, he saw a broken liquor bottle. He could smell its contents, like a stench.

The man whirled to the crowd of bystanders in a rage. "If I could just get my hands on the person who sold those kids that stuff," he yelled, "I'd *kill* him!" With that, he went back to his car and drove home.

After telling his wife the terrible news, he walked immediately to his liquor cabinet. If ever in his life he had needed a drink, it was right then. As he reached into the cabinet for his favorite bottle, however, it was missing. In its place was a sheet of paper, neatly folded. When he opened the paper, he saw these words in his daughter's own neat handwriting:

Dear Daddy,
We just wanted to celebrate tonight, so we borrowed your bottle. We knew you wouldn't mind!

Love, Emily

I don't know how you feel about alcohol. I know that believers have honest differences about its moderate consumption and what the

Scriptures actually teach. From my point of view, I saw enough of its ravages in my own childhood home to last a hundred lifetimes. Your experience might be very different. But the point of the story about the car crash is that one father took the example of his life too lightly. He claimed he knew how to handle liquor. He knew how to maintain moderation. He boasted that he knew how to drink without becoming drunk. But his young daughter and her date did not have that sophistication or experience. They died as a result.

In many ways our examples bring devastating results to the ones we love. Our actions speak so much louder than all of our words. And with a few acts we can deny or negate in a moment all that we've tried to set right.

Dr. Charles Howard, a marvelous professor from a Bible college in the Carolinas, told a story of going over to comfort a man whose son had just been killed in a terrible automobile wreck. The boy had been very drunk. When Dr. Howard arrived at the home to console the man, that grieving father grabbed him by the shoulders.

"Charlie," he said, "I killed my boy."

Dr. Howard tried to dissuade him. "No! You didn't kill your boy. On the contrary, you weren't even there. You had nothing to do with it. He was driving too fast, missed a curve, and struck a tree. He'd been drinking. He was careless. *You* had nothing to do with this!"

"Oh, yes I did, Charlie," the man replied, "because, you see, I taught that boy to drink. I taught that boy he could handle a drink. And now I've killed him. *I killed my boy.*"

Dr. Howard said there was nothing he could say to console the man. That father firmly believed that by example he had destroyed his own son, and would probably carry the weight of that grief to his grave.

TEACHING BY POSITIVE EXAMPLE

Like an interest-bearing financial account, a careless, thoughtless parental example can have compounding negative effects. In the same way, however, our positive example can grow in value for years to come. The dividends are great.

My wife, Betty, has always been the greatest example before the children. It is little wonder that they have all grown up wanting to be just like her in so many ways. She is proper and so honest in all her dealings. In every instance, no matter what it might be, this is a lady who always wants to "do the right thing."

At times, I've groaned inside when I think Betty is carrying that strict code of honesty to extremes. At many ball games, for instance, they'll let you in free at half-time. Assuming this to be true, the rest of us would just walk toward the open gate to get inside the ball park or gym before the second half. The only things I'd be thinking about would be the half-time score and the line at the concession stand.

But about that time we would hear, "Wait! Wait a minute! We need to buy tickets." And there she would be at the ticket counter, opening her purse, trying to purchase full-price tickets for a game half over. "But it's *free* now," we would tell her. "It's after half-time. We can go in now. Nobody cares." Even the person at the ticket counter would tell her, "It's okay. Don't worry about it. You can slip in now." But my wife would still try to buy a ticket, since it seemed the right and honest thing to do.

He didn't just "tell" us how to live, He left heaven's glory to show us the way.

Betty is the original Miss Squeaky Clean. But what a marvelous example she has been to the whole family. She believes integrity means faithfulness in the little things as well as the big things. There are times when I would like to be more "pragmatic," and bend a rule here or there to make it fit my lifestyle. But not her. She wants to walk the pathway as straight as she possibly can, one foot in front of the other, with no excuses or sidestepping. Everyone in the family loves and admires her for it, and always will.

Through the years we've both done our best to converse with our kids about integrity and moral purity. We've told them that compromise in any area of their lives would bring them pain. The children listened to us (most of the time), but they *heard* us when the consistent example of our lives truly matched our words.

THE ULTIMATE TEACHER AND EXAMPLE

You may have been one of those blessed men or women who grew up with a dad and mom who were patient, loving examples and teachers. Or if not one or both of your parents, maybe it was a grandfather or grandmother, aunt or uncle, pastor or coach.

On the other hand, you may never have had anyone like that in your life. Like me, you may never have had a dad who cared enough about you to tell you the secrets of life—or perhaps he was never around long enough to show you how to live by example. Perhaps you've grieved over that empty place in your heart, and feel that your life can never truly be complete.

My friend, we have a Father who is the ultimate Teacher. As marvelous and joyous as it may be to have an earthly dad to walk with us and show us life's ropes, our heavenly Father can be to us all that we ever need—and so much more.

When you think about it, it's wonderful and more than wonderful that He gave us His Word. Here is a Book that shows us how to live, how to prosper, what to avoid, how to respond to every situation in life—and even what our future holds.

You would think that giving us such an astonishingly complete Guidebook to live by would have been enough. But no, He didn't just "tell" us how to live, He left heaven's glory to walk with us and show us the way. Jesus Christ is "God in the flesh." As the gospel tells us,

> The Word became human and lived here on earth among us. He was full of unfailing love and faithfulness. And we have seen his glory, the glory of the only Son of the Father.... No one has ever

seen God. But his only Son, who is himself God, is near to the Father's heart; he has told us about him.[2]

The life of Jesus Christ gives us an Example like no other. He lived a life of perfection. He lived a life of love and sacrifice. In a thousand ways, both big and small, He showed us how to live in a way pleasing to God. He taught us how to go the second mile. He taught us how to forgive, and turn the other cheek. He taught us how to express compassion and care. He taught us how to view material possessions, and where true and lasting wealth may be found. He taught us how to face opposition, and how to stand for the truth when the whole crowd around us is going the other way. His every move inspires us. His death and resurrection redeem us. His every word explodes in our lives with meaning. As Scripture tells us, "He is the radiance of His glory and the exact representation of His nature."[3]

Jesus actually gives us the power to live as He lived. No earthly teacher can do that!

What a Teacher! What an Example! Many in our culture latch on to sports celebrities or movie heroes or music stars for inspiration. But Jesus Christ not only inspires us with His exploits and His example, He actually gives us the *power* to live as He lived. No earthly teacher can do that!

What more could our Father give us in addition to His Word and His Son? In the face of such staggering gifts, what more could He possibly do to teach us?

He gave us His own Spirit to live inside us and to be with us forever!
Jesus told His disciples,

"I will ask the Father, and he will give you another Counselor, who will never leave you. He is the Holy Spirit, who leads into all truth.... I am telling you these things now while I am still with you. But when the Father sends the Counselor as my representative—and by the Counselor I mean the Holy Spirit—he will teach you everything and will remind you of everything I myself have told you."[4]

Our own fathers may have ignored us, mistreated us, or even abandoned us. But here is a Father who tells us, shows us by example, and then—because He knows our weaknesses—actually comes to take up residence *within* us as a Teacher, Counselor, Mentor, and Friend. Here is an Instructor and Coach who leads us along at the best pace for us, since He knows us inside and out. He knows when to push. He knows when to put His arms around us and encourage. He is patient and long-suffering with our weaknesses, fears, and chronic failures. He never gives up on us!

And in those times when we are feeling unloved, incompetent, or unworthy, He whispers something in our ear, just as He led me to whisper in my own boy's ear so many years ago:

"My child, I want you to know that your Father is proud of you. He's just as proud of you sitting on the bench as He is when you're hitting home runs. I'm with you just as much in your failures and disappointments as in the high moments of success. There's no way I could ever be more proud of you. You're My own son—You're My precious daughter—and you don't have to do anything to earn My attention or My love or My grace. You've got it a hundred percent. I love you."

Chapter Nine

A Father Who Provides

No good thing will the LORD withhold
from those who do what is right.
O LORD Almighty, happy are those who trust in you. [1]

I n the early morning hours, along a dark stretch of California freeway, a highway patrolman pulled over when his headlights caught
something—or some*one*—in the median up ahead. As he aimed his
powerful spotlight at the chain-link fence in the center of the divider,
he could hardly believe his eyes.

It was a *child* standing there in the night—a tiny, frazzle-haired little
girl who couldn't have been more than four. She was clutching the
fence with her fingers, eyes wide with terror. She had gripped the wire
tightly for so long that the officer had to slowly and gently pry each fin-
ger loose, one at a time. As he spoke soothingly to her, while freeing her
little fingers, she looked up into the policeman's face.

"I don't think my mommy and daddy are coming back to get me,"
she said.

The thought of such a situation overwhelms me. How sad! How
tragic! How unbelievable! *"I don't think my mommy and daddy are coming back to get me."*

In fact, they weren't. The couple had put her out of the car and onto
the freeway median sometime after midnight, because they simply didn't
want her anymore. So she was abandoned, perhaps with the vague
thought that someone might see her and pick her up.

As you might imagine, when the story hit the media people responded from all over the United States and around the world. They offered to provide the little girl a home, and described how desperately they wanted a child like her. Almost anyone reading the gut-wrenching account would respond in the same way: How in the world could anyone abandon a precious little girl, so tender, so young?

There is more than one way to abandon a child.

Most parents, of course, would never consider doing such a thing. Even in our callous, often cruel culture, the idea that someone would just dump a little one alongside the highway like a sack of garbage seems reprehensible to nearly everyone.

But the fact is, there is more than one way to abandon a child.

PROVISION IS MORE THAN A PAYCHECK

Many parents are so preoccupied with their own pursuits and simply trying to "get ahead" or keep up with the Joneses, that they have not given their children the emotional provision and tender watch-care they need. Some men in particular feel their parenting task is complete when they bring home a paycheck. That's not to in any way diminish the financial aspects of providing for a family. Working hard to keep food on the table and the rent paid is an honorable, commendable, *manly* activity. And God will honor that effort.

But financial support is only a beginning! Without a father's guidance, care, protection, and *presence,* a child may actually grow up feeling as though he or she has been abandoned along the highway of life—no matter how much money Dad brings home!

As you've learned in the pages of this book, I too was forsaken by my mother and father. My father left before I was born, caring nothing for me. And my mother was so desperate that she listed me in the classified ads, seeking to place me with a family who could care for me. But looking back now, as a man in my middle years, I can make the same statement that David made: "Even if my father and mother abandon me, the LORD will hold me close."[2]

Due to the influence of Pastor and Mrs. Hale on my life during my first five years—and undoubtedly also to the faithful prayers that followed me through my days even after I was taken from their home—I grew up believing I could and should make a way for myself. I did not sit back and say that the world and society owed me a living. I did not wait for the government or for welfare to care for my mother and me. Nor did I go out and try to take from others what I did not have. I began working hard at the age of twelve, setting money aside whenever I could. As long as I can remember, I've always believed that if I worked hard, I could truly get ahead.

When I became a Christian as a young man, I discovered a deep well of confidence such as I had never known. Suddenly I had something I never had before…a Father-Provider! Many people have mistakenly said through the years, "James, you have so much self-confidence." I know why they might say such a thing, but in reality it wasn't *self*-confidence at all; it was *God*-confidence. With all my heart I believed my Father God could do anything. And since He had become my Abba-Father and "Daddy" in life, I believed He would provide for me in every way and show me how to "make my way prosperous and have success," just as He told Joshua.[3]

Some men feel their parenting task is complete when they bring home a paycheck.

Far too many men are abandoning their role as provider, refusing to accept responsibility. Psychologists tell us that this is the result of inadequate training in their own homes, and in most instances results from the missing role model of a father in their lives.

How do we overcome this vital missing member of the family unit? With all my heart I believe that by coming to know God as Father and by studying His Word, we will discover that He *is* our provider "who richly supplies us with all things to enjoy."[4] Not for one moment does this imply that we're to be materialistic in our thinking. But if our heart and focus are right, we *can* enjoy "all things," whether those things are many or few.

THE ULTIMATE PROVIDER

Have you ever stopped to think what a difference it would make in the world if everyone knew God as Father and Provider? People scheme and strive, fight and claw, and pour out their lives to get the basic "stuff" they need for life—things such as food, clothing, and shelter.

Greed drives many people to cheat, rob, and steal—even when they have all the material things they really need. But what is behind that greed? Most likely it's a fear of not having enough. They go on scratching for more and more because, depending on their own ability to provide, they can never quite feel secure with what they have. Somehow, it's never "enough."

Jesus tells us that our Father-Provider sets us free from this emotion-sapping struggle for survival. He tells us:

> "Don't worry about having enough food or drink or clothing. Why be like the pagans who are so deeply concerned about these things? Your heavenly Father already knows all your needs, and he will give you all you need from day to day if you live for him and make the Kingdom of God your primary concern. So don't worry about tomorrow."[5]

If people would obey this and believe in Him, what a tidal wave of peace would sweep across our world!

The psalmist wrote: "For the LORD God is our light and protector. He gives us grace and glory. No good thing will the LORD withhold from those who do what is right. O LORD Almighty, happy are those who trust in you."[6]

Solomon observed: "It is a good thing to receive wealth from God and the good health to enjoy it. To enjoy your work and accept your lot in life—that is indeed a gift from God."[7]

Paul reminded his friends: "This same God who takes care of me will supply all your needs from his glorious riches, which have been given to us in Christ Jesus."[8]

One of the most profound truths my Father-Provider has shown me through the years is that the way to "get ahead" and open doors in life is by being a servant. If we are looking out for others, rather than inward upon ourselves all the time, we will discover a richness in life beyond anything we have experienced. This mindset runs directly counter to the spirit of our age! Yet it is as true as the morning sunrise. The more you work to help others succeed, the more you will find yourself secure, established, and at peace in your soul. When you have a genuine interest in the joy, happiness, and lasting success of others, you will find that your own life becomes rich with a wealth that has very little to do with bank accounts or stock portfolios. You will be rich in friendship.

Even if my father and mother abandon me, the LORD will hold me close.

As I write these words, I can't help but think of the story of a woman named Tabitha. We read about her in the Book of Acts. She was such a giving, loving, caring person, "always doing kind things for others and helping the poor."[9] When she became ill and died an untimely death, her friends and the people of that little town of Joppa simply *would not let her go*. They pulled in the apostle Peter from other duties he was tending to in a nearby town, and all but demanded that he raise her from the dead! Standing around the woman's body in an upper room, everyone was talking at once and kept shoving garments under Peter's nose—articles of clothing lovingly sewn and given away by Tabitha.

Peter finally chased them all out of the room, dropped to his knees by the body, and asked the Lord to raise this good woman from the dead. He was probably thinking in the back of his mind, *I saw Jesus raise the dead. I must be sensitive to God's will in this situation, just as Jesus was.* Here was a woman so loved, so appreciated, so valued, so rich in friendship that her friends took on Death itself, saying, "We can't let her go! She's ours! We love her." And God in His sovereign will saw fit to raise her, to give her life again.

A LEGACY OF GIVING

Many people have commented on how much joy I seem to derive from seeing others have a good time. I have a lot of fun in life, and much of it comes from watching others have fun. It's almost as enjoyable for me to see one of my friends or family members land a big largemouth bass while fishing as it is for me to do it. (I did say "almost.")

My own children have learned this major life lesson. They too have found great pleasure in helping others find provision and happiness. In turn, they are giving their own children so much more than mere material, financial provision. They're giving them *direction.*

He is our provider, "who richly supplies us with all things to enjoy."

My good friend Dennis Peacocke teaches seminars on "how to do business God's way."[10] And one of the most important aspects of what Dennis shares is the difference between materialistic "riches" and true, authentic wealth.

Dennis points out that many people gain "riches" only to have them slip through their fingers because of a self-centered, indulgent lifestyle. I can't help but think about a few of the players on our former world-champion football team here in the Dallas-Fort Worth area, the Dallas Cowboys. Just recently, it seems that player after player has thrown away his "riches" and his future because he didn't know how to live! Some of these athletes have been blessed with almost superhuman skill and wonderful personalities, yet they have lost their possibility of lucrative endorsements and hurt their own team (not to mention their families) by selfishly putting their own pleasures and lusts before all else. As Paul wrote: "Their god is their appetite, they brag about shameful things, and all they think about is this life here on earth."[11]

Dennis Peacocke notes that if you have riches and then lose them, you probably will be unable to regain them…unless you have *wealth*. A person who has wealth will most likely be able to regain a measure of financial success, should he lose it for some unexpected reason. This is because true wealth (which is a depth of character) will produce riches. A truly wealthy person will not have his or her focus on amassing toys or property or piles of money, but rather on personal productivity and helping others.

Real biblical wealth is the capacity to produce with the focus on benefiting and providing for others. This is the way of God our Father-Provider and Christ our Lord. Jesus cared about pleasing His Father, and continually showed His deep concern for the needs of others (though He Himself did not have a place to lay His head at night).

If you are reading these words as a parent or grandparent of small children, I pray you will come to understand the importance of imparting true wealth to those under your sway and influence. Let them know that love does not give in order to get. Rather, it is a genuine desire to promote the other person's best interests. When we learn to love in this way our return is "inexpressible and glorious joy."[12]

Our Father's provision goes far beyond material things. He also gives Himself to us as an Encourager! He tells us that He has given us "everything we need for life and godliness."[13] Have you ever heard the expression "Get a life"? That is often made in reference to people who seem to live life at such a substandard level that they merely exist. They're only taking up valuable space! Yet Scripture tells us Jesus Christ didn't come to us saying, "Get a life," He came to *give us life* and give it to us more abundantly.[14] And we will experience the beautiful fullness and sweetness of that life as we pour ourselves out on behalf of others.

A JOY BEYOND ALL OTHERS

I can't adequately describe to you the deep joy and the treasure-house of memories we have experienced in our ministry since we began caring for the hungry, the hurting, and the suffering throughout the world.

Have you ever seen children who have nothing—and I don't mean "little," I mean *nothing*—wait in line for hours just to get a bowl of soup? They stand in line longer than American children wait in lines for rides at Six Flags or Disneyworld. When you look at the faces in those amusement park lines, they often don't look very "amused" or excited. But little children who have been hungry all night and all day are so happy waiting for a warm bowl of soup. Their little faces absolutely light up when they see you coming. You can't believe those smiles! Why? Because they're so grateful! They know you are coming to them

The way to "get ahead" and open doors in life is by being a servant.

with life itself in your hands. And at the same time, it is *life for you* to be sharing the love of Jesus and helping them in that way!

We in the Western world have been so spoiled. Our understanding of the very nature of life has been so distorted, warped, and perverted. People throw away their few short years on earth running after some will-o'-the-wisp they call "happiness." They become like a little child chasing a butterfly but never able to catch it. They become like fools chasing a mirage of water in the desert until they collapse with thirst. People pursue and pursue until they are exhausted with the effort, yet all the while they are *missing life.*

And it is LIFE that our Father-Provider offers us! True life. Authentic life. Overflowing life. Not some gilded, gaudy Hollywood imitation. And every person can have it! God tells us that if we want to experience life, we must learn to share life.

We call our daily television program *LIFE Today*. And we make reference to the fact that we *are* sharing life today. This isn't just a title to put into the TV listings; we're asking the viewers of our program to join us in sharing life today and every day.

I love Paul's straight talk to some folks who had lost their focus and forgotten what life was all about. He may have written these words two thousand years ago, but they are surely as relevant and appropriate today as on the day he penned them for his young friend, Timothy:

> Tell those who are rich in this world not to be proud and not to trust in their money, which will soon be gone. But their trust should be in the living God, who richly gives us all we need for our enjoyment. Tell them to use their money to do good. They should be rich in good works and should give generously to those in need.... By doing this they will be storing up their treasure as a good foundation for the future *so that they may take hold of real life.*[15]

PROVISION DOESN'T MEAN A LOTTERY

It has broken my heart to see how many people in the Christian community have twisted our Lord's words in the Sermon on the Mount to accommodate their own agendas. Jesus said, "Give, and it will be given to you. A good measure, pressed down, shaken together, and running over, will be poured into your lap."[16] Yes, our Father-Provider will certainly take care of us as we seek to meet the needs of others. But some would turn these words into some kind of spiritual lottery game: Give God money (preferably to such-and-such a ministry) and you'll have a money tree spring up in your back yard. Just go out in your driveway with a bushel basket and wait for that currency to fall out of heaven.

The more you work to help others succeed, the more you will find yourself secure, established, and at peace.

God does indeed provide in miraculous ways, and He delights to bless His children in every way. But the person who truly has the heart of his Father-Provider doesn't just give with the hope of getting. He does so for the sheer *joy* of it. For that matter, the promise of Luke 6:38, the passage just quoted, comes out of a context of giving mercy and forgiveness to others. It really isn't even talking about money. As we extend grace and mercy to others, it will come back to us with heavenly dividends!

But in our materialistic, money-minded age, we immediately apply the "give and it shall be given unto you" to that which will fatten our wallets. Yet we need to remember that God, who graciously commits Himself to meeting our needs, has clearly told us to be satisfied with food and clothing and shelter.

We need to ask God's Spirit to recalibrate our hearts. We need to ask Him for eyes that look right through the glitter and tinsel of counterfeit riches to see the true wealth that our Father-Provider has in store for each one of us.

Then, once we finally see as He does, we need to take our children by the hand and show them, too.

Chapter Ten

Who You Are
to the Father

How great is the love the Father has lavished on us,
that we should be called children of God!
And that is what we are![1]

JOHN

I magine yourself slowly regaining consciousness in a strange room. As the darkness rolls back, your eyes begin to adjust to your surroundings. *Where are you?* You look slowly from side to side. Try as you might, you can't remember how you came to be in such a place. It's a hospital room—you can see that much. But where? How? Why?

Gingerly, you examine your hands and wiggle your toes to make sure you're "all there." Yes, everything moves. There is no pain. No bandages or visible wounds. As though waking from a dream, you wait for that odd sense of disorientation to dissolve and return you to reality.

But this time, reality refuses to return. With a growing sense of panic you realize you can't remember...*anything.* You not only don't know where you are or why you're there, you don't know *who* you are.

What could be more frightening than amnesia? To know that you have a family...a home...a history...loved ones somewhere...a place where you belong...*but it's all out of reach!*

I don't know how common the sort of disorder just described might be. But there is another type of memory loss suffered by those who follow Jesus Christ and belong to the heavenly Father. It's an amnesia I've suffered from myself at times in my life.

SPIRITUAL AMNESIA

In the Bible, Peter wrote about a group of Christians who had experienced a strange, collective memory lapse. Noting that they were no longer advancing in their walk of faith or seeking to know their Father, Peter said of them: *"They have already forgotten that God has cleansed them from their old life of sin."*[2]

It's easy to become distracted from our faith and forget who we really are…

—when the world presses in;

—when daily pressures and anxieties weigh us down;

—when hopes and dreams crumble and leave us discouraged;

—when the flesh fills our mind with fantasies;

—when mundane duties crowd out thoughts of heaven;

—when pride turns our eyes from all we owe Him.

Before Moses died on the borders of the Promised Land, he used his last words to deliver a strong warning to the people of Israel. Unless they were very, very careful, he told them, they would slip into spiritual amnesia and *stumble into disasters worse than the slavery they had escaped.*

"Be careful! Beware that in your plenty you do not forget the LORD your God…. For when you have become full and prosperous and have built fine homes to live in, and when your flocks and herds have become very large and your silver and gold have multiplied along with everything else, that is the time to be careful. Do not become proud at that time and forget the LORD your God, who rescued you."[3]

Fifteen years ago, I discovered just what a distracted man I had become. It was like waking up from years of spiritual amnesia. And the strange thing was, I had been feverishly occupied in "the Lord's work" when the reality of my life in Him began to slip away. The sad fact was, I'd become a high-flying, big-time preacher who no longer loved God with all my heart. Yet when I finally opened my eyes and realized what was happening to me, I seemingly turned my back on what many people have said was the greatest evangelistic career ever.

Friends told me that if I announced my failures, shared about my battles with lust, and began speaking outside mainline Baptist circles, I was writing off my future. Not only that, but in those first days after coming out of my "amnesia," the devil told me I could never find my way back to my first love—that I could never have the kind of fellowship with the Father I'd cherished as a boy and young man.

I'd become a high-flying, big-time preacher who no longer loved God with all my heart.

Looking back now, it's difficult to believe I could become as blind as I did during those intense, barn-burning days of my nationwide crusades. I remember trying to catch my breath a little as I sat at a table during a precrusade dinner. I'd already spoken in six states that week, and life was rushing by in a kaleidoscope blur. Sitting near a lady at my table, I gradually became aware that she had been trying (unsuccessfully) to make conversation with me.

"Brother Robison," she was asking me, "when do you pray?"

My answer came right off the top of my head. I looked at her and said, "Ma'am, I haven't got time to pray. Tell you what. I'll preach...*you* pray."

I remember feeling good about that answer. I even repeated the conversation to some friends. "I told that lady how I pray!"

How far I had fallen from that intimate walk with my Father. I'd broken faith with Him. I hadn't kept the commitment I'd made back in Bible college to love Him with all my heart. In the midst of some of the greatest ministry I could have ever imagined, my heart had drifted from simple fellowship with Him. I'd forgotten who He was to me...and who I was to Him.

WAKING UP

During that time, I remember being introduced to a country preacher out in one of the communities where we were holding a crusade. I couldn't help noticing how poorly the man was dressed—holes in his shoes, an old, wrinkled-up shirt, a patch on the knee of his pants. Yet the man gripped my hand warmly in his own callused hand and said, "Brother Robison, I'm honored to meet you. We've got thirty people in our congregation, and we pray for you all the time."

Something about the man touched me. "Thank you, sir," I told him. "I appreciate that a lot."

Well now, I thought as I got into the car, *wasn't that nice?* As an associate pulled the car out onto the highway, it was as though God tapped me on the shoulder and began asking me a series of uncomfortable questions. Have you ever experienced anything like that? Have you ever sensed God's Spirit probing deep within, touching your innermost thoughts?

"James, did you see that man's shoes?"

"Yes, Lord. I saw. They had holes in 'em."

"Do *your* shoes have holes in them?"

"I don't think so."

"He didn't have a very nice shirt on, did he?"

"No, Lord. No, he sure didn't."

"What kind of shirt have you got on?"

"It's a nice shirt, Lord."

"You've got nice suits, too, don't you?"

"Yes, I really do."

"How many people does he preach to?"

"About thirty, Lord."

"And how many do *you* preach to?"

"I don't know. I'm told millions."

Then God got to the point of the conversation. "Do you know something, James?"

"What, Lord?"

"*That* man loves me with all his heart, and you don't! And you make me sick!"[4]

I literally began to weep. I laid my head on the dash as my friend watched. I cried out to God, "Please help me to fall in love with You again...like that preacher does."

Sometimes I've felt as though there was never a preacher who disappointed God like I did. I was so consumed with trying to be the man everybody *expected* me to be that I forgot who my Father had *called* me to be.

Through most of my years of young manhood, I was trying to find out who I was. It seemed like I wondered and worried about it through so much of my life. My own dad never helped me, never showed me, never told me. I really never even knew him. As a result, I found myself looking for fathers everywhere I went. I'd come alongside older men in the course of my ministry and— without saying anything—I'd find myself thinking, *Would you be my father? Would you help me to know who I am?*

The devil told me I could never find my way back to that first love.

How defeated I was. And even after I was delivered from this terrible state of amnesia,[5] Satan kept telling me I could never go back, I could never again enjoy the Father and walk with Him as I once had.

It was a lie! The truth is, you *can* return to your first love. You *can* awaken from your amnesia and remember that you belong to the heavenly Father. You can come back to your true home, your true family, your true purpose in life, and your true citizenship.

But not without a fight! Not without a struggle! The enemy will do everything he can to distract you from this relationship; he'll throw up every roadblock he can think of to keep you from enjoying that personal, intimate relationship with your Creator and Savior. The devil will even use seemingly positive things—in my case, a national evangelistic ministry—to distract you from a close, loving relationship with your Father. Paul the apostle warned of this: "I fear that somehow you will be led away from your pure and simple devotion to Christ, just as Eve was deceived by the serpent."[6]

I'd forgotten who He was to me . . . and who I was to Him.

In those moments of struggle and warfare and "identity crisis," it's good to take out your eternal ID card to review a few vital statistics. It's helpful to pull your adoption papers out of the file and remember again just *who you are, Whom you really belong to, and why you are where you are.*

In case it hasn't dawned on you lately, you have a Father who loves you with a love that soars beyond your ability to understand, imagine, or conceive.

The closest we can come to understanding this Father's love comes in our experience as parents. The following experience, related by Gordon Dalbey, makes clear those special feelings between a father and his child.

After a year, when the late-night nursings were beginning to exhaust my wife, Mary, I knew it was time for Dad to take over. But I'm a heavy sleeper. I didn't look forward to being awakened randomly at night. "I don't know how you do it," I'd often said to Mary.

Now it was time to find out.

I confess I balked at nighttime feedings partly because John-Miguel, a little over one year old, always awoke crying "Mommy!" I felt like a second-fiddle mom—and not a very good one at that.

In fact, I started out as more hindrance than help. John-

Miguel's cries were not loud enough to awaken me, but they did wake Mary, who soon learned that only a well-placed elbow in my side would bring me to consciousness.

The elbow and the relentless cries for "Mommy!" were not pleasant motivators, and with that first nighttime whimper I began bargaining with the Lord. I prayed. I begged. I was ready to deal. *Please, Lord, make him sleep! It's better for the baby, after all. I'll pray for an hour a day. I'll increase my tithe!*

But still the cry for "Mommy!" went on.

Yawning, I rolled out of the sack and stumbled into John-Miguel's bedroom. *Maybe it won't be so bad after all,* I told myself. I took a deep breath. "Daddy's here!" I announced hopefully. "It's okay!"

To my pleasant surprise, the room fell silent. *Well, that wasn't so hard!* I thought and confidently stepped toward the crib.

"MOMMMYYY!" Shattering my eardrums along with my ego, the cry blasted forth with renewed vigor. Startled, I stopped—then sighed. Gingerly, I picked my boy up and put him on my shoulder.

Week after week, bottle after bottle, I pushed on through the cries for Mommy—dutifully, if not lovingly. Soon, however, I began to enjoy just holding my little son. Before long, I was praying for him, even singing my prayers softly at times. On a few especially tough nights, we walked out onto the patio, under the stars, and talked about moons and dogs and raisin bread.

And then late one night, it happened.

Lost in heavy sleep, I stirred as a strange sound tapped lightly on my ear.

"Daa-dee…"

My eyes flickered open, closed again. Shifting, I reached to pull the covers higher.

"DA-DEE! DAA-DEEEEE!"

Bold and full-throated, the small voice pierced the dark morning stillness like a bugle.

My eyes exploded open. Lurching from the bed, I raced into John-Miguel's room and scooped him up in my arms. "That's my man!" I cried, laughing and lifting him high above my head. "Hallelujah! That's my man!"

"What's going on in there?" Mary called out sleepily from our bedroom. "I didn't even wake you up, and you're in there making all that noise!"

Sheepishly, I lowered a confused and bleary-eyed John-Miguel to my chest. "I'm not sure...exactly what's going on," I called back. "But...it's okay. I mean, it's good."

I held my son against me at last and smiled. "*Real* good," I whispered, shaking my head. "Real good."

What, indeed, stirred—even leapt—within me that night when I first heard my son cry out "Da-dee!"? Certainly my joy came partly from waiting so long for him to acknowledge the bond between us. And yet, when I had rejoiced fully, and both he and Mary were asleep again, I lay in bed staring at the ceiling in awe, gripped by something deeper.

I was identifying with the cry of my son. In his baby's voice, I heard something I recognized in myself. I believe every man harbors that cry deep within his masculine soul. It's the primal, human cry for security and saving power in a dark and broken world: "Save me, Daddy!"

Before Mary and I had children, my best friend—a father of two—told me, "Nothing will help you understand the love of God like having a child of your own."

He was right.

May we fathers dare listen to the cry for "Daddy" in our own hearts so we can recognize it in our own children and respond in love. That's how we witness to them about the Spirit of God, who saves us from fear and "makes us sons, enabling us to cry 'Abba! Father!'" (Romans 8:15, New English Bible).[7]

Paul, trying to get that point across to some friends, said: "May your roots go down deep into the soil of God's marvelous love. And may you have the power to understand…how wide, how long, how high, and how deep his love really is…though it is so great you will never fully understand it."[8]

He wants you to spend time with Him, to learn to know Him as your own Father and Companion. He wants the very life of His Son to pulse in your veins and radiate from your life in a steady blaze of reflected glory. You and I, then, must make sure that *nothing* distracts us from the simplicity and purity of devotion to Jesus and the Father. And if we do find our grip on eternal realities beginning to slip—if we find ourselves beginning to forget what real life in Him is all about—it is time to review again just who we are to this Father who purchased us at such an unbelievably high price. In the next few pages, let's take a few moments to do just that.

Who are we to Him?

WE'RE HIS REBORN CHILDREN

The Bible says that when we trusted Christ as our Savior, we were born into God's own family! We became members of His very household. Listen…

God has given us a new birth because of His great mercy. We have been born into a new life that has a confidence which is alive because Jesus Christ has come back to life. We have been born into a new life which has an inheritance that can't be destroyed or corrupted and can't fade away. That inheritance is kept in heaven for you, since you are guarded by God's power through faith.[9]

In my late teens, while living in the home of the Hales, I was able to see for the first time how a real father lives and relates to his children. After I married Betty and our own children came along, I was privileged to experience the joy of becoming a daddy myself. Being a father—and now a grandfather—has helped me more than anything else to understand something of the Father's love.

Betty and I enjoy sitting by the hour watching our children and grandchildren as they relate to each other and to us. They're all the entertainment we need! Our hearts well up with gratitude when we see them doing things together and enjoying one another. *There is nothing more gratifying, warm, and secure in life than a family ruled by love.* And, of course, God intends His household to be such a family.

God fulfills to the utmost a father role as sire, as name-giver, and as our link to both the past and the future. No one born spiritually into the great family of God need ever suffer from an identity crisis or from confusion concerning origin or destiny. No earthly father could begin to give the assurance in these matters that the heavenly Father provides His children.

WE'RE HIS CHOSEN ONES

In any family we're accustomed to speaking of children as either "naturally born" or "adopted." But in God's family, we're *both*. Just in case we should ever doubt our parentage, the Bible says we have been born into His family—and adopted, too! He wants us to understand and never forget that we were *chosen*.

As Paul explained it: "Long ago, even before he made the world, God loved us and chose us in Christ.... His unchanging plan has always been to adopt us into his own family by bringing us to himself through Jesus Christ. And this gave him great pleasure."[10]

I've often thought about this matter of God's adoption. My wife Betty and I have two beautiful daughters who were born to our marriage union. What a joy they are! But between those two daughters, we discovered that Betty had a medical problem that made it seem unlikely she would be able to bear another child. Later, she was miraculously healed of that condition.

In the meantime, however, we adopted a baby boy. Randy.

Our love for Randy fills our hearts every bit as much as our love for our daughters. It is unique and special. As the years went by and the time seemed right, I explained to Randy how we adopted him. As I did, I read passages of the Bible where God tells us how we have *all* been adopted as His own dearly loved spiritual children.

Randy is our son, our delight, and an heir with his sisters of everything we have. How grateful we are that we were able to choose him as our own!

As I've already mentioned, I can remember the hurt of being a strange boy in a new neighborhood and never being picked for a team when the kids chose up sides. I'd just turn and walk away because I didn't get picked, or at best was picked last. It hurt! But God *always* picks us. He picks every one of us. God chooses His children.

> *I was so consumed with trying to be who everybody expected me to be.*

As a prospective adoptive parent, you might walk into an orphanage and say, "I'd like that little boy (or little girl)." Yet there are cases on record where a couple chooses the child, and the child refuses to go! For whatever reason, he or she refuses the adoption.

I believe it's the same when God walks into the orphanage of our broken world. He has the desire and the capacity to adopt us all![11] He could and would take every one of us home…if we were all willing to receive His salvation and go with Him. He has made provision to save and forgive the whole world.[12] He has enough love to go around. He has the house. He has the room. He has the heart. He has the desire. He has the parenting skills. He has the time.

But sadly, many men and women refuse to become His children.

They refuse the adoption, preferring to be orphaned and alone in their lives—right into eternity. Nevertheless, the truth remains: No matter who you are, no matter what your background or history, He has chosen you for adoption! As Jesus said to His disciples, "You didn't choose me. I chose you and appointed you to go and produce fruit that will last."[13] He didn't leave you out. He didn't leave you standing alone. He chose you and He loves you.

WE'RE A YOUNGER BROTHER OR SISTER OF JESUS

Born and adopted as we are into God's family, we have Jesus Christ, the mighty Son of God as a big Brother! The Bible says:

> Jesus, who makes people holy, and those who are made holy are from the same family. So he is not ashamed to call them his brothers and sisters.[14]

If you are a Christian, you are a brother or sister of the Lord Jesus. You are as much a part of the family of God as Jesus Himself. The Bible says "we are heirs together with him."[15] God has provided you with all the credentials you need to establish your identity, your "roots," and your purpose in life.

WE ARE HIS DWELLING

Before you received Jesus as Savior and began to know God as Father, you probably thought of God as a Being who lived far away from you. Even many Christians, years after being born again, feel there is a great distance between them and their Father.

But this is not true. God has welcomed us into His very presence through Jesus. He invites us to come boldly to Him. What is even more electrifying, though, is the thought that *our Father has come to live with us*. He has actually made us His dwelling place through the Holy Spirit, who lives in us. Listen to these astonishing words...

God is building a home. He's using us all—irrespective of how we got there—in what he is building. He used the apostles and prophets for the foundation. Now he's using you, fitting you in brick by brick, stone by stone, with Christ Jesus as the corner-stone that holds all the parts together. We see it taking shape day after day—a holy temple built by God, all of us built into it, a temple in which God is quite at home.[16]

WE ARE HIS FRIENDS

Jesus, who came to earth to reveal the Father, said: "You are my friends if you obey me. I no longer call you servants, because a master doesn't confide in his servants. Now you are my friends, since I have told you everything the Father told me."[17]

If you had an earthly father who was a good provider and protector and who disciplined with love and fairness, you were blessed. But the best fathers are those who, in addition to all this, are also good friends to their children.

A friend is someone who is "there" when you need to talk about things that are bothering you, "there" when you want to share some-thing exciting or celebrate some accomplishment, "there" when you need a listening ear, a hug, or someone to say, "I understand."

God is just *that* kind of Father and Friend to you.

WE ARE HIS WITNESSES

Back in the Old Testament, the Lord told His people, "I am the LORD, and there is no other Savior. First I predicted your deliverance; I declared what I was going to do, and then I did it—I saved you.... You are witnesses that I am the only God."[18]

When some Christians think about "witnessing," they picture accosting strangers on the street or knocking on door after door like a traveling salesman. But God never intended us to think of being His witness as some kind of grim, grit-your-teeth "duty."

I can remember being around a group of kids in school when one of them would say, "Hey, guess what my dad did!" And the other kids would be all ears while this boy told how his dad caught a big fish or took him to the circus. Then one of the other boys would pipe up and relate something *his* dad had done. Not to be outdone, every kid in the group would have to tell something about his or her dad.

Without realizing it, these kids were being witnesses of their fathers. A witness is simply someone who tells what he has seen, heard, or experienced. And when you know God as your Father, you will do that. You won't think of it as "duty." You will be so proud of your *Abba* Father that you'll tell everyone you meet everything about Him. ("Hey, did I tell you about what my Father did for me yesterday?")

WE SHARE OUR FAMILY'S CALLING

What is the meaning of life? Why are we here? Questions like these keep those outside of Christ feeling bewildered, wandering, and unfulfilled. They live out their days with a void in their lives. No degree of success, no amount of money, no height of fame or prestige can ever fill that void, because life has no real meaning or driving purpose for them.

For that very reason, *understanding our calling as God's children is one of the most gratifying aspects of the salvation we receive in Jesus Christ.* The Bible says He has a "high calling" for us. There is nothing greater or more noble. Yet it is attainable even for the least of those in the kingdom of God—because it is guaranteed to us by His promises and His mighty power.

What is this high calling? Paul expressed it like this:

We know that in everything God works for the good of those who love him. They are the people he called, because that was his plan. God knew them before he made the world, and he decided *that they would be like his Son* so that Jesus would be the firstborn of many brothers.[19]

His calling is for us to be molded, shaped, and conformed to the image of Jesus, God's firstborn Son. And within this great, general calling, God has specific missions and assignments for each of us individually. You will experience great joy in discovering, pursuing, and fulfilling your part in God's heart!

REMEMBERING WHO WE ARE

As a Christian, you are part of His family, and heir to all that has been promised to Jesus. Your heavenly Father loves you unconditionally. He is an attentive daddy who is always willing to listen and encourage you. He has forgiven you and cleansed you. He is not keeping a record of your failures, only your victories in Jesus.

Your Father wants to help you find your way through life. He knows the questions of your heart and your soul's deepest needs. He sees when you are afraid, lonely, angry, hopeless, or despairing. He wants you to know His peace and to walk in confidence. He wants to show you His perfect plan for your life, and to empower you as never before.

> *Your Father knows the questions of your heart and your soul's deepest needs.*

Your Father is a never ending source of life, hope, provision, and protection. He is a great and mighty Deliverer. He will teach you everything you need to know and correct you when you go astray. He is your strength when trouble comes, and your Light in the darkness. He asks you now to live in a way that will bring honor to His name.

You can enjoy the blessings of your loving heavenly Father *today*. Why not reach out now and take His hand?

Perhaps you've had a sad, difficult life. But I want to tell you that in Jesus, the Father accepts you and wants to use you, right *where* you are, just *as* you are. I saw a beautiful example of this recently on our ministry's television program. Roger, a pastor from Fort Worth, told how he had been saved and delivered from a life of fatherlessness. His father hadn't physically abandoned him, he just never showed much care or concern for his son. When his boy needed him, this father was never there.

As a result, yet one more young man grew up without a role model...and never learned how to become one. Roger gave little or no attention to his young daughter and son. Eventually, as a teen, his daughter rebelled. Within a few years she died of a drug overdose in a distant city. And Roger's relationship with his son was so angry and bitter that at one time he even plotted the boy's murder.

But then Roger met his Father. Through Jesus Christ he found a healing, transforming relationship with God. Now, as a pastor, husband, and father, he pours out his life to see other lives mended. He works through a rehabilitation home with men whose lives have seemingly been shattered beyond repair—often as a result of their own fatherlessness.

But Roger knows better than to write off anyone's life as "beyond repair." He has a Father who can fix anything! The biggest miracle of all in Roger's life occurred just recently, when he was privileged to lead his own father to Jesus Christ and Father God.

God has miracles in store for you, too. He wants to make you into a lighthouse of hope, light, and love in a bitter, unhappy world.

And it all begins with the realization that you are accepted and loved by your heavenly Father.

Chapter Eleven

A Father Who Works for My Good

"As far as I am concerned, God turned into good what you meant for evil. He brought me to the high position I have today so I could save the lives of many people. So don't be afraid."[1]

JOSEPH, TO HIS BROTHERS

A s a father, and now a grandfather, I have a deep desire in my heart to see good things happen in the lives of my children and grandchildren. I want to be there for them, encourage them, and do whatever I can for them. I want to see their lives grow strong and flourish. It's part of my father's heart toward them. My own father, consumed as he was by alcohol from an early age, never developed a father's heart. There was no room in his thoughts for concern about the good of his son. Trapped by his addiction, he could only think of himself and that next bottle.

In God, we have a Father who thinks of us unceasingly. We are never absent from His thoughts. As David wrote, "How precious it is, Lord, to realize that you are thinking about me constantly! I can't even count how many times a day your thoughts turn toward me."[2] And this is a Father who not only desires to see good in my life, He has the will and power and wisdom to cause it to happen!

But what does that really mean? Does it mean I will never experience tragedy in my life? Does it mean I will somehow escape the heartache and pressure, the grief and bruising, so common to man? Does it mean that?

No, God never promises that our lives will be free from pain and hurt and disappointment. But He *does* promise to work everything to our good.

EVEN IN LIFE'S DEEPEST HURTS

The deaths of two little children, coming within a few days of each other, have grieved and shaken our ministry family here at Life Outreach International.

Nine-year-old Tiffany appeared recently on our television program, *LIFE Today*, in a segment called "Children Fighting for Their Lives."

God never promises that our lives will be free from pain and hurt and disappointment.

Suffering with a terminal disease, this precious little pastor's daughter touched a national audience with her courage, faith, and sweet, patient spirit.

Here at the ministry, we prayed and wept and agonized over Tiffany's long illness. People in her daddy's church family prayed continuously for her, even spending the night on their knees in the family's front yard. So many prayed that Tiffany might live; and in all truth she *does* live. She's more alive than ever before, but now in a better place—in the presence of her Lord.

In the same period of time, another family very close to ours watched their precious three-year-old boy Adam slip out of this life, joining Tiffany in heaven with Christ. This, too, hit us all a hard blow in the heart. We've all been hurt so deeply over these deaths. For a time, it seemed as though I would go to bed at night weeping and wake up weeping in the morning. Perhaps you have walked the same road recently. Perhaps through some hurt or tragedy or pressure in your life, you too have come to the place where you've said, "I don't know if I can bear this. I don't know if I can take this anymore."

The truth is, none of us is immune from the trauma of tragedy and death. It is a fact of life that in this lifetime we are going to face suffering, pain, and sorrow. Scripture affirms again and again that man's days are short and—in so many ways—filled with trouble. Jesus Himself told us, "In this world you will have trouble."[3]

Even so, I've encountered people who struggle with this fact; they seem to think that if a person is right with God and serious about following Him and doing His will, they will never have to face this sort of adversity. But that's simply not so. Good and godly people suffer right alongside those who have rejected the Lord and live only for themselves.

Most of us understand those things, at least to a degree. But somehow the death of a child pushes the issue to a whole new level. To see one of these tender, innocent ones suffer and die so young can make us all want to cry out, *"Why?* How could God allow this to happen?" Some would even blame and accuse God, saying, "If He really is God, if He really is all-powerful and in control, if He really is a loving Father, then why doesn't He do something about this? Why does He let such tragic things happen?"

"Why?" is perhaps the most natural question.

But I've been learning to ask a different question.

Not "Why?" but *"What?"* Knowing that I have a Father who loves me and who is able to turn even my tragedies into triumphs, I am learning to look into His face and ask, "What is this all about, Father? What do You want to do as a result of this? What is Your purpose? What is Your eternal perspective on this? What good can come of this thing? What should I do or become because of it? What effect should this have on me and those I love?"

A passage often quoted to us in times of heartache or tragedy is Romans 8:28. Because we've so often heard this verse quoted mechanically or without feeling—almost as a cliché—we sometimes dread to hear it. Even so, there is great help and deep meaning in this passage, if we take time to understand what our Father is truly saying to us.

And we know that in all things God works for the good of those who love him, who have been called according to his purpose.[4]

Notice how this verse begins.

"AND WE KNOW..."

It doesn't say "we think," "we wish," "we surmise," or "we sincerely hope." The Bible says we *know*. There are some absolutes here. The culture we live in today doesn't appreciate the idea of absolutes or absolute truth. They don't like being told, "This is the way things *are,* and there is no changing it." They're not comfortable with Ten Commandments; they would prefer having "Ten Suggestions."

Yet in our Father and in His Word, there are absolutes. Things that never change, never move, never falter, never fail, never fade, never evolve into something else. There is comfort in this fact alone. This is a Father who does not change. And when He makes a promise, you never have to wonder if He's going to forget about it or change His mind. For that reason, we can say with confidence, *"We know."*

What do we know?

"IN ALL THINGS..."

"We know that *in all things* God works for the good of those who love Him."

Because God is God, He's involved in everything that happens. Because He is sovereign, nothing takes Him by surprise. He knows everything. He has foreseen everything. And He isn't just sitting back watching it all unfold. He is not a passive Father, He is involved. He works with events in our world. He works with events in our lives. And through it all, He accomplishes His purposes.

In the processes of life itself, within this creation on a broken, sin-damaged planet, there are forces that God permits to move forward. There is a continuous inner shaking within this changing, unstable world of ours. There are earthquakes and floods, droughts and famines, tornadoes, and blizzards. In addition to these forces of nature, there are things that directly plague humankind: disease and aging and pain and physical deformities.

These things trouble *all* of us. Your picnic can get rained on. Your house can be swept away in a flood. Your plans can be interrupted by adverse weather or illness or a traffic accident.

You may say, "Well, I want to make a commitment to God or some kind of decision in my life that will prevent me from facing these things." My friend, that simply won't happen in this lifetime.

Because of mankind's rebellion at the beginning of time that severed his relationship with the Creator, these hurtful things are facts of life. A little earlier on in Romans chapter 8, Paul tells us that Creation itself groans in pain and frustration over its present condition. Everything that God has made looks forward to and yearns for the day when the Creator will liberate His creation from the instability and hurt and decay of this present age.[5]

He is not a passive Father. . . . He works with events in our lives.

In addition to these things, we must also endure the direct and indirect consequences of sin that have been unleashed in our world. Someone driving down a street shoots randomly out the window of a speeding car. The bullet passes through a window of an apartment and into the body of a little child at play in his bedroom. A drunk driver careens head-on into a carload of teenagers coming home from a youth meeting at church. A godly missionary woman is brutally raped in her own home. A retired couple are bilked out of their life savings by a fast-talking, crooked investor. Good people are hurt by the sinful actions of others! As residents of this world, godly men and women—and yes, children, too—must sometimes share in that harvest of pain and hurt.

That's the bad news. But there is good news, too.

"GOD WORKS FOR THE GOOD..."

What does the passage say? "In all things God *works for the good* of those who love him." In the midst of it all there is a God who sovereignly weaves these events—even the results of sin and the acts of sinners—into a pattern for good in the lives of His children.

We might wish His mission in our life was to "stop all the bad." But that's not our experience, and that is not what the Scripture says. Instead, He is causing all things, good or bad, joyful or hurtful, happy or tragic, to work together for ultimate good.

Now "good" may be the furthest thing from the mind of someone who would deliberately hurt you or wound you. He or she may intend evil against you. The enemy, the destroyer, the

The Lord loves to turn Satan's evil plans and attacks right back on his head.

powers of darkness may hatch plots, shoot fiery arrows, and bring events into your life intended to harm you or break you or drag you down. But God intends to work it all for good. And He has the power to bring it about.

Filled with hatred and envy, Joseph's brothers threw him in a pit and later sold him into slavery. But God had a marvelous redemptive plan of action that brought about great good for many people. At the end of it all, Joseph could say, "As for you, you meant evil against me, but God meant it for good, in order to bring about this present result, to preserve many people alive."[6]

In the midst of my deep hurt for the parents and family of that little three-year-old boy who died recently, God worked for good in my own life—as well as the family's. If only you could have seen what I saw when I walked into little Adam's funeral. I saw the glory of God in the countenance of that little boy's mother and father. I don't know how else to describe it. When I looked at this beautiful, grieving mom, I saw the Prince of Peace and the glory of God. I beheld a miracle. By all logic, that mother's face should *not* have been radiant. And yet it was! At that

moment, in the darkness of her sorrow, she was experiencing the wonder of God's sustaining grace—working adversity, pain, suffering, and
loss for good and for eternal gain. I could see the same result in the dad
and grandparents.

What I saw that day changed my life, just as being with that little
boy had touched me so deeply and profoundly. I sent a note to the family later in the week which read, "Your little Adam changed my life.
Your family changed my life." That was no exaggeration. It was fact.
Through the life and death of that child, my life was impacted in a positive way for the rest of my time on earth—and for eternity. I wanted to
shout out loud at that funeral: "This little one changed my life!"

No, I was not the one who took the direct hit in that painful experience. That mother and father, those brothers and sisters, those grandparents—they're the ones who took the direct hit. But there have been
direct hits in my life through the years, and I have no doubt more will
follow. Yet in spite of that fact, I am determined to throw all the pain
from such blows right back in the face of the enemy, the destroyer. My
desire is to torment him by showing the glory and majesty of our ade-
quate, sufficient Savior Jesus, who is greater than the pain and the problems. Come whatever may, in "all things" I am going to magnify the
Lord.

As Paul wrote, "God is able to make all grace abound to you, so that
in all things at all times, having all that you need, you will abound in
every good work."[7]

The Lord loves to turn Satan's evil plans and attacks right back on
his head. I think of Stephen, in the Book of Acts. The Jewish leaders
hated him for his clear, ringing testimony for Christ. The Bible says
"they could not stand up against his wisdom or the Spirit by whom he
spoke."[8] And since they couldn't prevail against him or silence him,
they decided to kill him. As he was being stoned to death, he looked
up and saw the Lord Jesus in heaven, standing on the right side of
God—ready to receive Stephen into heaven. Bloodied and dying, his

last words were, "Lord, do not hold this sin against them."[9]

Now how was the Lord "working for the good" of this young man who loved Him? The hate was not good. The stones were not good. Stephen suffered greatly, and his friends and loved ones "mourned deeply" for him.[10] Yet Scripture indicates several things that happened on that day.

First of all, Stephen's last moments—even in his pain—were bathed in great glory. He was full of the Holy Spirit, and heaven itself opened up to his wondering eyes. He saw his dear Lord Jesus standing at the right hand of the Father (I believe Jesus gave him a standing ovation), and soon his spirit was soaring into those loving arms. What a welcoming party! Stephen was filled up with God's glory and God's comfort in that greatest crisis of his life. God was with him in his pain, and filled Stephen up with Himself.

God's ultimate will for our lives is to be conformed to Jesus.

Second, a young man named Saul of Tarsus was there, witnessing it all. He saw the way Stephen died. He heard Stephen cry out to God to forgive his tormentors. And I believe something happened in Saul's heart that day. I believe that Saul came under such conviction by the Spirit of God that he began to run. And running toward the testimony of Jesus to destroy it, he ran into Jesus Himself. When the Lord appeared to him on the road to Damascus, his heart was prepared and ready to respond. Saul the persecutor of Christians became Paul the apostle, the greatest Christian to ever walk the face of this earth.

A third thing happened, too. Scripture says that on that very day, beginning with that incident, a great persecution broke out against the church, and believers "were scattered throughout Judea and Samaria." With that scattering, the gospel spread like wildfire across the land. New churches were established and thousands entered the kingdom.

Satan, who delighted in the death of Stephen, saw his plans turn upside down. God worked through that awful attack and brought incalculable good to His people and to the world. He used it to glorify the name of His Son.

"CALLED ACCORDING TO HIS PURPOSE"

I want you to notice something else. The passage says that "in all things God works for the good *of those who love him, who have been called according to his purpose.*" He does not promise here to work for the good of everyone. He does not promise to work for the good of those who are in love with themselves, in love with the world, or in love with success and pursuing their own way. He does not work for the good of those who would raise a clenched fist toward heaven and shout with Frank Sinatra, *"I did it MY way!"*

This promise is specifically directed toward those who love the Lord and who recognize that He has called them to a specific mission and purpose in life. What is that purpose, you ask? We don't have to wonder about it. God tells us clearly in the very next verse.

For all the people who so glibly quote Romans 8:28, you find very few who go on to quote Romans 8:29! Yet they are part and parcel of one another. Here is what it says:

> For those God foreknew he also predestined to be conformed
> to the likeness of his Son....

What is His purpose in our lives? That we might be conformed into the image of His Son! This is the will of God. This is the great purpose and plan of God in your life and mine. Do you know what it means to be "conformed"? It means to shape something into an image, just as a sculptor shapes a hunk of clay. In another passage, Paul tells us, "Do not conform any longer to the pattern of this world."[11] Why? Because God's ultimate will for our lives is to be conformed to Jesus Christ.

Have you ever watched a sculptor at work, how he prods and

bends and smoothes that clay until it begins to resemble something or someone? Out of that shapeless mass a form begins to emerge, and you suddenly recognize it. You say, "Oh! I know what that is. That's a bear (or a deer or a shepherd or the face of Abraham Lincoln)."

The clay must give under the pressing fingers of the artist. It must yield.

That's what God is doing in your life. He's shaping you. He's molding you. He's forming you into an image…and it is the very image of His Son, Jesus Christ. You are called according to this purpose.

If an artisan is working with a certain type of rock and it cracks or crumbles under his chisel, it will never be perfected. Nor will an artist work with clay that is hardened and dried. Clay has to be pliable. Bendable. Moldable. Submissive. It must give under the pressing fingers of the artist. It must yield.

God is shaping us in the same way. He is taking all of the pressures in life that squeeze us, push on us, and press in on us, and He is using those very things "for good." And what is the greatest good? That people might catch a glimpse of the face of Jesus, just as I did that day at Adam's funeral. That people might see in your life and mine the Author of Life, the Prince of Peace, and the Good Shepherd, who laid down His life for the sheep.

Remember, we are to be expressions of His light and His life. The most radiant and reflective of all jewels is the diamond…and diamonds are formed under some of the most intensive pressure on earth!

CRAWLING UP IN GOD'S LAP

Just a few days ago, I was sitting in my den, my face in my hands, broken-hearted for these families who'd lost little ones. The phone rang and it was my daughter Robin on the line. She, too, was feeling the pain and loss. She has a little boy almost the exact same age as Adam.

We were talking to each other on the phone, sharing that pain together as father and daughter, when God suddenly spoke to my heart, as clearly as He has ever spoken to me. God was saying, "James, the longing that you and those families feel for the little ones who have died, that's how I long for you. In these moments when you feel so much love in your heart that you'd just do anything to help these hurting ones, that's how I feel about you every moment of your life. You can't even grasp how much I love you—how I long to hold you."

With tears spilling over and running down my face, I said to my daughter, "Robin, God wants me to get into His arms—right now. Robin, you know how you hold your little babies and they just snuggle up against your shoulder and hold onto you? That's how God wants me to fit into His arms. He wants me to just melt into His arms of love. This is what He feels for His children all the time."

In those tender moments, I felt that God was also telling me something about His heart for the world. He was telling me that if I would allow the pain in my heart to make me be yielded and submissive to Him, I could begin to feel what He feels toward His own children—and beyond that, to a lost and dying world. And just as we grieve when a killing disease strikes a little child, so God grieves over the sin that destroys homes and families and lives. I began to see the horror and ugliness of evil as I had never seen it before. It is a hateful thing; a killing thing.

But through it all, He wants His children to shine like lamps in a dark place. As we allow the pain in our lives and the hurt in our world to shape us into the image of the Savior, a great good is released. A great light blazes forth.

People see the face of Jesus in your face.

People see the life of Jesus through your life.

People find the hope of salvation in Jesus through your response to the pain and suffering common to all of us.

And that's not only "good," it is the best thing that could ever be.

Chapter Twelve

Reaching Out
to the Fatherless

"For in you the fatherless find compassion."[1]

HOSEA

It is very easy for me to understand the pain, loneliness, disappointment, and lack of direction in the hearts of those who have grown up with an absent or abusive father. Having grown up without my father, I understand the fatherless.

But from that day as a teenager when I came to know God as my Father, my love for the fatherless has almost overwhelmed me at times. It's as though God's great heart seeks expression through my own.

Putting feet to that deep concern, I traveled for more than thirty years speaking in crusades, and at junior high and high school assemblies. I communicated with teens in more than 1,200 assemblies; it was amazing to see the response of the students.

As I would conclude my challenge during assemblies, I would make very strong remarks concerning morality, purity, and mutual respect between boys and girls. Though many heard and responded, I knew there would always be some kids in their immaturity who would use the occasion to laugh and mock.

So I would wrap up my talks with words like these:

"Remember this, young men and women. Some of you may walk out of this assembly making fun of me. You may even mock me. That is your choice. I can't do anything about that. But I do want you to keep one thing in mind. One day a man came to your school to speak. No one paid him to come—not one dime, not one penny. He had nothing to gain by coming. He came for only one reason. He came because he cared about you."

You could almost feel those words hitting home across the auditorium. After that, even the kids who wanted to act smart didn't dare. And if some did, the other kids stopped them in their tracks and said, "Knock it off. That man only came because he cared." They could see that I really did care. And it was a life-changing experience for thousands and thousands of young people throughout North America.

> *As a fatherless man, I understand the fatherless.*

I literally worked myself into exhaustion trying to tell kids about a Father who loved them. I wanted so much to help them. I longed to see their lives changed. I also wanted to see the lives of fathers and mothers changed so that they could become more devoted to their children and to their God, as well as to one another. Seeing families turned around has been one of the richest experiences of my life.

And when that change comes—when we begin to love our Father as He loves us—we will in turn love and reach out to others.

Jesus said that when you touch the hungry, the hurting, the suffering, the naked, and those in distress, you actually touch Him.[2] If we want to minister to God we must minister to those He loves and longs after. We must reach out to the fatherless in the Father's name.

THE FATHERLESS AMONG US

Fatherlessness has been a great destroyer in our culture. Many if not most of our nation's social problems today can be traced directly or indirectly to fathers who aren't there—or who aren't being the kind of fathers God intended them to be.

But there is hope in Jesus Christ. There is hope in the heavenly Father. And in an increasingly fatherless America, we have an unprecedented opportunity to bring people to a knowledge of the true Father. And please hear me in this: *They're hungry for it. They're looking for it.* But they don't want religion! They want something with substance. Something that goes home with them. Something that touches everything they do and everything they are. Something that's *real*.

And that's what Jesus is. He is real. He is present among us. And He is the only way to the heavenly Father. He gives us eternal life and brings us into a personal, intimate relationship with the God who loves us so dearly.

Whether they realize it or not, that's what people are looking for. When men, women, and young people join cults and gangs or become involved in immoral or destructive lifestyles and habits, they're only looking for something to fill the awful void they feel inside.

God has a heart to bring these individuals to Himself, but it doesn't stop there. He wants those whom He has adopted as His own to reach out to others in His name and in His power. He wants the word out: There is an open invitation to join God's family.

No one can impact society more effectively than people with the Father God's heart. We are those people.

An Opportunity

I am personally convinced that believers should consider the fatherless condition of so many Americans as a choice opportunity for winning the lost to Jesus Christ. Of course fatherlessness is deplorable. It's destructive. Satanic. God never intended His plan for fatherhood to be disregarded or destroyed. Fatherlessness is simply the work of the devil, whose strategy is to counteract God's efforts to reveal Himself to humanity as a loving Father.

But we also know from the Scriptures that God is able to transform the most terrible evils into that which advances His good and loving plans. When, for example, Joseph's jealous brothers sold him into slavery in Egypt, they clearly meant it for evil. But as Joseph pointed out to them later, "God intended it for good."[3] He used Joseph's slavery and ultimate rise to power in Egypt to save Israel during a famine that could have wiped that little nation from the face of the earth.

In the same way, God in His mighty sovereignty can use America's tragic state of fatherlessness to accelerate His outreach to the lost in the waning days of this millennium.

Fatherless people are searching for a father! For THE Father. What a glorious opening this presents for Christians to lead people to their heavenly Father, the loving Creator and God of the universe! What a marvelous opportunity to say to a lost nation, "Here, my fatherless friends, here is the true and living One who has been searching for you longer than you've been searching for Him!"

Unless we're a living demonstration of the Father's love, we're just too much talk.

In the past few decades, evangelical believers have become much more active in politics and the affairs of government. As our nation slides further and further away from God, alarmed Christians have organized and become more politically sophisticated. They're voting, polling, canvassing, lobbying, and running for office in unprecedented numbers.

Yet even while all this is happening, our nation's crime rate, abortion rate, illegitimacy rate, murder rate, and divorce rate continue to soar unchecked. Our society is coming unraveled before our very eyes. As Judge Robert H. Bork writes, we are "slouching toward Gomorrah."[4] So what is the answer? Ultimately, *it is not political,* even though Christians certainly ought to vote and take an active role in their government.

The only lasting answer for our country is for children of the Father to know Him as He wants to be known, and live for Him as He calls us to live. The answer is to so demonstrate the abiding, overcoming power of an occupying presence in our lives that it flashes a beacon of hope to a world under the foot of the enemy. It gives them courage to believe there might really be a way to overcome those habits and circumstances of life that drag them down and push their face in the dust.

Our lives need to become so attractive and so magnetic that people look at us and say, "They've got something you can't get at the casino even if you win the jackpot. They've got something money can't buy."

They've got to *see* it in us, not just read it on our bumper stickers or hear us talk about it in church. They need to see it in our neighborhoods, in our schools, at our workplace, and wherever we go. And it must be *real*. Reality with a capital "R."

Yes, as Christians we will at times side with unpopular causes, fight for what is right, resist evil, take our stand in the public square, and speak the truth in love. *But unless we're a living demonstration of the Father's love, we're just so much talk.* We won't make any difference in the lives—earthly and eternal—of the people around us.

You see, the very heart of our nation has been separated from God as Father. We may still vaguely acknowledge Him as a supreme being, but we don't know Him as Father anymore. A personal, intimate relationship with the Creator of the universe is almost unknown across our land. That is the very thing *we* must demonstrate in our lives. That's what will make people around us say, "What must I do to be like you?"

Peter tells us to "always be prepared to give an answer to everyone who asks you to give the reason for the hope that you have."[5] Those words imply that our hope ought to so flame within us and seep through every pore of our bodies that people *can't help* but notice!

THE ONE WHO CONVINCES

When we look at some of the unlovable, fatherless people around us, we're often inclined to doubt that they can, let alone will, turn to God the Father. We struggle to visualize them *ever* accepting Christ as Savior. They seem too hard. Too deep into sin. Too deaf to spiritual truth. Too preoccupied. Too self-satisfied. Too sophisticated and cynical. Too engrossed in their pursuit of pleasure. Too wrapped up in false doctrine.

But here's the good news: We don't *have* to persuade people to accept Christ! We don't *have* to talk them into recognizing God as their heavenly Father or argue them into doing so. And we couldn't do so even if we *wanted* to!

The Christian's role and privilege is to simply present the true gospel—to lay it out for people to see. Jesus told the disciples, "You shall be My witnesses."[6]

When we have been faithful to that calling, we must then simply trust the Holy Spirit to perform His work in those who will respond to His call. Jesus said, "No one can come to me unless the Father draws him to me."[7] He also said, "If I am lifted up from the earth [crucified], I will draw all people toward me."[8]

The Word of God, wielded by the Holy Spirit, is able to pierce the hardest armor.

As Christians, we're to proclaim the truth of the crucified and resurrected Jesus Christ. But only the Father and Jesus Himself can draw the lost out of darkness into the light of the gospel. And the Agent who does the work of the Father and the Son in drawing people to Christ is the Holy Spirit.

Christians should not witness except in the power of the Holy Spirit; that is, in a condition of being completely yielded to Him and trusting in Him to do His work in men's and women's hearts.

Just before He went to the cross, Jesus described in some detail what the Holy Spirit would do.

"When the Helper comes, he will prove to the people of the world the truth about sin, about being right with God, and about judgment. He will prove to them that sin is not believing in me. He will prove to them that being right with God comes from my going to the Father and not being seen anymore. And the Helper will prove to them that judgment happened when the ruler of this world was judged."[9]

As witnesses of the gospel, we are not the ones who bring sinners under conviction. We can't do it! No matter how heart-touching our presentation, no matter how logical our arguments, no matter how classy our materials, we *cannot* convince them that righteousness is available through Christ and a loving heavenly Father. We can't persuade them that rejecting salvation, bought and paid for by the blood of Christ, will bring judgment and eternal punishment.

But, praise God, we don't have to convince them! That's the Holy Spirit's job. Our task is simply to place in the Spirit's hands the instrument He uses to get His work done—the living Word of God.

The Book of Hebrews tells us that "God's word is alive and working and is sharper than a double-edged sword. It cuts all the way into us, where the soul and spirit are joined, to the center of our joints and bones. And it judges the thoughts and feelings in our hearts."[10]

Christians don't have to worry about the spiritual hardness of their lost friends, neighbors, and relatives. They don't have to trouble themselves over seemingly impossible situations. The Word of God, wielded by the Holy Spirit, is able to pierce the hardest defensive armor. It "discerns" the wickedness of the sinner's heart and reveals that darkness to him as he has never seen it before.

People cannot be saved until they are made to realize how utterly lost they are through this convicting, persuading, proving work of God's own Spirit.

Through our words and through our lives, then, we must be His instruments to touch a fatherless nation. But the world is so much larger than our national borders! And God, who cares very little about such boundaries, has a heart for the fatherless of this whole hurting world.

THE FATHERLESS OF THE WORLD

Years ago when I was speaking at a crusade in South Africa, I met an evangelist and humanitarian who would have a tremendous impact on my vision for a wider fatherless world. His name was Peter Pretorius. Together we went out to Soweto, one of the very depressed areas of Johannesburg. We saw the poverty; we saw the crushing need. Yet Peter told me that as severe and serious as these conditions were, they *paled* in comparison to areas where he was working in Mozambique.

"James," he told me as we walked those dusty streets together, "did you know that I can give starving children a nutritious, vitamin-enriched soup mix and in six months stabilize their health? In many instances, we can save their lives."

"That's remarkable!" I said. "What does it cost to feed a child?"

"I can feed a hungry child for $1.50 a month."

I was really taken aback. "Do you mean to tell me," I said, "that you can feed a child for six months for about *ten dollars?*"

"That's exactly right, James. It's not total child care, but it does give them nutrition—and it does save their lives. I wish you and your wife could go with me and see what we see."

A few months later, Betty and I did just that. We participated in a huge evangelistic crusade in Mozambique, and it was marvelous. Over 10,000 accepted Christ in just a matter of days. As a matter of fact, I spoke on one of the nights and they told me that nearly 5,000 people made commitments to Christ on that night alone.

But even more exciting was the love investment that made it all possible—Peter's faithful, efficient work among the hungry. We toured devastated areas where we saw hungry, even starving, children. We went into areas where warring factions had caused hundreds of people to flee their homes and villages. We saw huddled masses—families of five, six, and more—too weak to even walk. Little children were dying every day in the villages.

Then Peter took us into areas where they had been feeding for a few months—and already you could begin to see the changes.

You could see the children's complexions clearing, their little faces brightening. The feeding program was obviously working! Not only was it saving lives, but it was making huge openings for the preaching of the gospel. The wide-open opportunities to proclaim the Father's love were staggering to me.

Since Life Outreach International began participating in relief efforts less than ten years ago, African officials tell us that we have helped save the lives of more than two million children. We currently feed 65,000 children a month, moving from one hard-hit, devastated area to another, once the children's health is sta-bilized. We also have a maintenance program in almost every area to make certain that they do not regress.

This is a father who will love us through eternity.

There have been more than three million professions of faith in the areas where we have reached out to the hungry and the hurting. A number of months ago, we asked Peter Pretorius to go into Rwanda to minister to refugees after nearly half a million people died in that nation's unbelievably horrible civil war. Some say that more people may have died in Rwanda than in any war in human history.

Peter found his way to the community of Gitarama, not far from Kigali. As seasoned a relief worker as he was, Peter was staggered by what he saw. He told us that he had *never* seen or even imagined so many orphans. Estimates of the number of children without families exceeded 100,000. A young Rwandan expatriate, Fred Nikanda, was trying to care for as many of these children as he possibly could. Peter asked me to come over and see how Fred had housed hundreds of them in an abandoned Catholic church school.

"Please come see these children," Peter said to me. "They're beautiful. They're precious. But James—they've been devastated! In most instances, their parents were brutally murdered before their eyes—with bullets, machetes, and clubs. Many of the children are scarred physically and have wounds from the slaughter. They *all* carry emotional and psychological scars."

So I flew to Rwanda with our ministry team, and went to see the orphanage. It was yet another life-shaping experience for me. We began to get actively involved in caring for these children. On that first trip, we actually had to empty our pockets of expense money and leave it with Fred. That burdened man had completely exhausted his resources and didn't know where to turn. Brokenhearted, he was about to leave the area because he could no longer care for the children or pay any workers. We left him with enough money to get by a while longer—until I could get back home and ask people for emergency help.

We're now building a very large orphanage in Gitarama, on land that the government donated because of the work we are doing. The orphanage can care for more than a thousand children. They're truly some of the most beautiful boys and girls I've ever seen. They will not allow anyone to call them "Hutus" or "Tutsis," the names of their warring tribes. Instead, they put their arms around one another and say, "We are family. We will not use those names." Many of the older children have embraced Jesus Christ as Savior—as have virtually all of the workers.

Who would have thought there could be so much beauty coming out of Rwanda's years of hell?

In November 1996, Fred Nakunda died suddenly of undiagnosed diabetes, at the age of thirty-three. It was heartbreaking. We decided to name the orphanage after Fred. He had literally become an expression of the Father's heart to the fatherless.

As a result of Peter Pretorius's Rwandan refugee work in neighboring Goma, Zaire, doors were opened for him to begin speaking in large public meetings. Zaire is a huge country with a vast population and many problems. As a direct result of the work in Rwanda and the crusades that have opened in neighboring Zaire, we have already seen more than 1.3 million professions of faith in Christ. More than twice as many people have come to know God as Father as a result of our going to Rwanda than died in the civil war. The only hope for nations like this is the true knowledge of God and His redemptive love.

We have been invited to come speak and minister in some of the first public meetings that will ever be assembled in Rwanda as peace takes hold. I believe that in that country alone, more people will come to know Christ than died in the war.

God has a heart for the fatherless of this whole hurting world.

The fatherless and motherless are all around us.

I believe that if every one of us would find ways to demonstrate God's heart, we would find life's greatest fulfillment. Whether or not we had a father who was the proper role model is no longer the issue. By committing our life to God through faith in His Son, Jesus Christ, we now have the greatest Father in the entire universe!

This is a Father who will love us through eternity.

This is a Father who will direct our steps.

This is a Father who will enlarge our hearts.

This is a Father who will give us the capacity to touch the lives of the suffering and fatherless.

What a heritage! Let's spend the rest of our lives sharing this Father's love. Many of the most effective, dynamic witnesses for Christ I have ever met are men and women who grew up with poor or nonexistent father role models. Yet they became some of the strongest, wisest, most loving husbands, wives, fathers, and mothers. They may not have had fathers, but they came to know the ultimate Father.

In Him, they found all that they need. And so can we.

Jesus said to His followers, "He who believes in Me, as the Scripture said, 'From his innermost being shall flow rivers of living water.'"[11]

Wherever rivers flow, life springs up. As you receive His love and His life, release that refreshing reality toward others, remembering these words of our Lord Jesus: "It is more blessed to give than to receive."[12] What a Father we have to know and to share.

Let's tell the world. Let the river flow.

Questions
for Discussion

CHAPTER 1
MY FATHER'S FACE

1. What goes through your mind after hearing about James Robison's childhood and father?

2. How was your experience with your own father similar to, or different from, the one James described? How did that shape who you are today?

3. In what ways has your relationship with your earthly father affected your perceptions of your heavenly Father?

4. Read Matthew 6:6–9. Why do you suppose God has chosen to call Himself our Father?

5. Read John 1:12. What would you say it means to be God's child?

6. James longed for a father who would encourage, accept, and never leave him. He found that Father in God. What do you need most from a father? How might your heavenly Father meet that need this week?

CHAPTER 2
A FATHER WHO IS THERE

1. Reread the brief story at the beginning of this chapter. What do you think motivated those prison inmates to send cards to their mothers—but *not* to their fathers?

2. Do you agree or disagree with this statement: "A father has no greater gift to give his children than time"? Defend your answer.

3. The conference speaker referred to on page 36 tried to substitute money for his presence with his son. What do we sometimes try to substitute for our presence with our children?

4. What does it mean for a father to know his child? How does a father do that?

5. Read Isaiah 46:3–4 and Psalm 139:7–12. God is a Father who is always there. What does that mean to you? Be specific.

6. When do you feel too busy to spend time with your heavenly Father? What can you do about that this week?

CHAPTER 3
A FATHER WHO LISTENS

1. Who is the best listener you know? What makes that person a good listener?

2. Why have we all been created with a longing to be listened to? How do we attempt to fulfill that longing?

3. Read Psalm 18:6 and Psalm 40:1. James pictures God as a daddy leaning down to hear His child speak. What image comes to your mind when you picture God listening to your prayers?

4. Read Psalm 31:22. When do you feel like God has stopped listening to your prayers? How do you respond during those times?

5. What tempts you to neglect God's ever-present, listening ear? What happens when you give in to that temptation?

6. What can we do this week to help each other take advantage of having a heavenly Father who always has time for His kids?

CHAPTER 4
A FATHER WHO TALKS TO ME

1. When has an encouraging or instructive word from a friend or family member really made an impact on you?

2. Why do you suppose we're "poor receivers" when it comes to hearing God speak?

3. Describe a time when the Bible seemed to speak directly to you, communicating exactly what you believe God wanted you to hear.

4. Read Psalm 32:8 and John 10:1–5 and 10:14–15. How do you listen to God?

5. Have you ever felt like God was using a dream to communicate with you? What happened?

6. Read Jeremiah 29:13–14. What can we do this week to follow the instruction of this passage? How will that help us become better "receivers" of the messages God wants to speak to us?

CHAPTER 5
A FATHER WHO LEADS ME TO THE BEST

1. Who are your role models? What makes you admire and want to emulate them?

2. What hopes and dreams do you have for your children? How are you using your influence as a role model to help them fulfill those dreams?

3. Read Jeremiah 29:11. How does it make you feel to know your heavenly Father has dreams for your future? Explain.

4. What dreams do you have for your future that you believe are part of God's plans for you?

5. Have you ever felt like you were "getting in God's way" as He tried to lead you in a certain direction? Describe that time.

6. What can you do this week to gain a better understanding of (and commitment to!) your Father's plans for you?

CHAPTER 6
A FATHER WHO APPROVES AND ACCEPTS

1. What comes to your mind when you search your memory to find experiences of approval or acceptance?

2. As a boy, James needed a father's encouraging approval to help him when it came time to choose baseball teams. When do you need your heavenly Father's approval most?

3. Why is a father's approval—or lack of it—so influential in the lives of both sons and daughters?

4. How does God communicate His acceptance and approval to you? What difference does that make in your life?

5. Read Ephesians 1:3–8 and 2:6–7. How can these scriptures help you the next time you feel unloved, unaccepted, and like a failure?

6. What can you do to remind yourself each day this week that your heavenly Father loves, accepts, and approves of you?

CHAPTER 7
A FATHER WHO CORRECTS

1. What goes through your mind when you see another person's child throwing a tantrum in a public place? How does your perspective change when it's your own child?

2. How would you explain the difference between "training" a child and "telling" a child? Why is that distinction important?

3. Read Proverbs 13:24; 19:18; 22:15; 23:13–14; and 29:17. What methods of correction work best in your family?

4. Read Hebrews 12:10–11. How does God correct you, His child?

5. What can we learn about God's loving correction from the example of Jim Bakker described on pages 104–106?

6. In what ways do you sense God is gently correcting you, calling you to return to Him this week?

CHAPTER 8
A FATHER WHO TEACHES

1. Finish these sentences: "A patient teacher is..." and "A patient father teaches..."

2. What have you learned from the failures of others? What do you want your children to learn from your failures?

3. In what ways is a father's example like an interest-bearing financial account? Be specific.

4. James describes his wife, Betty, as someone who has been a positive example of honesty and integrity to him and his children. Who has been a positive example for your family?

5. Read John 1:14 and 1:18. How would you describe the example God has given us in Jesus Christ?

6. What's one thing you can do this week to follow Jesus' example in the way you relate to your family?

CHAPTER 9
A FATHER WHO PROVIDES

1. What was your reaction when you first read the statement, "There's more than one way to abandon a child"? Why did you react that way?

2. When have you felt like an abandoned child?

3. Read Psalm 27:10 and Philippians 4:19. How has God provided for you in the past? What kind of provisions do you expect Him to make for your future?

4. What are ten ways God could use you as His tool to provide for someone else's needs?

5. How does a person pursue "wealth" rather than "riches"?

6. What needs to change in order for you to better "share life" with those around you this week? How will you initiate that change?

CHAPTER 10
WHO YOU ARE TO THE FATHER

1. In what ways has "spiritual amnesia" affected you in the past month?

2. When was the last time you truly felt like your heavenly Father loves you with a love beyond your comprehension?

3. Read 1 Peter 1:3–4. How would you describe the "inheritance that...can't pass away" to someone who has never heard of it?

4. Read Ephesians 1:3–5. In what ways has (or could) being adopted into God's family changed you personally? Be specific.

5. Read Ephesians 2:20–22 and John 15:14–15. How would your life be different if God were not present in it?

6. What's the most important thing you've learned from this chapter? How will that impact your attitudes and actions this week?

CHAPTER 11
A FATHER WHO WORKS FOR MY GOOD

1. How might your daily life change if you really came to grips with the fact that God is thinking about you unceasingly—every minute of every day?

2. Look up John 16:33. What three "facts of life" does Jesus give us in this verse? Describe the balance between "good news" and "bad news" in our Lord's words here.

3. What might be the difference between asking God why He has done something as opposed to what He might be doing in our lives?

4. What connection do you see between Romans 8:28 and Romans 8:29?

5. In your own prayers, do you find yourself more often asking God to "stop the bad" or to "work it all for good"? How might that change as you grow to maturity in Christ?

6. How did God work Stephen's terrible murder for "good"? When you meet Stephen in heaven, what's the first question you might like to ask him?

7. Looking back on your life, what are some of the key "bad things" that happened to you which God eventually worked "for good"?

CHAPTER 12
REACHING OUT TO THE FATHERLESS

1. What do you think it means to have a heart for the fatherless?

2. Who has been a "living demonstration of the Father's love" in your life? What can you learn from that person to help you be a living demonstration of God's love in the lives of others?

3. When is it difficult for you to trust the Holy Spirit to bring about a heart-change in the lives of those to whom you are a witness?

4. Why do you suppose so many people in Mozambique, Rwanda, and Zaire have been so responsive to the gospel message?

5. The orphanage in Rwanda is a living testimony of Fred Nakuda's heart for the fatherless. If you were to leave this world tonight, what kind of testimony would you leave behind?

6. What's one truth you've gained from your time in this book? How can you use that to help you touch the lives of the fatherless around you from now on?

NOTES

Chapter One

1. Psalm 27:8, NKJV

Chapter Two

1. Psalm 27:10, NLT
2. Adapted from a story by Ken Canfield
3. Isaiah 9:6, NKJV
4. Isaiah 46:3–4, NLT
5. Psalm 139:17–18
6. Psalm 61:3, NIV
7. Psalm 145:18–19, NLT
8. Psalm 37:4, NLT
9. 2 Corinthians 1:3–4

Chapter Three

1. Psalm 116:1–2, NLT
2. Chuck Swindoll, *Killing Giants, Pulling Thorns* (Portland, Ore.: Multnomah Press, 1978), 33.
3. Genesis 2:20, NLT
4. Genesis 2:18, NLT
5. James 1:5, *The Message*
6. Psalms 18:4–6, NLT; 31:22, NLT; 34:6, NIV; 40:1–2, NLT; 65:2–3, NIV
7. See Romans 8:26–27.

Chapter Four

1. Psalm 32:8, *Modern Language Bible*
2. Proverbs 25:11, NCV
3. John 10:4.
4. John 4:4, NIV
5. See John 10:1–5, 14–15.

6. Romans 10:17, NASB
7. Proverbs 1:20–24, NLT
8. See 1 Peter 1:13; 4:7; 5:8–9.
9. Jeremiah 29:13–14, NCV

Chapter Five

1. 2 Corinthians 5:7, *The Message*
2. Adapted from Jeremiah 29:11–13
3. Jeremiah 17:5,7, NCV
4. Psalm 139:1–4, NCV
5. Romans 12:1–2, Phillips
6. Romans 12:3–4, Phillips
7. 2 Corinthians 5:7, *The Message*
8. Isaiah 30:21, NIV
9. Proverbs 4:18, NIV

Chapter Six

1. Isaiah 43:1, NKJV
2. 1 Thessalonians 2:11–12, *The Message*
3. Adapted from Ephesians 1:3–8; 2:6–7, NLT
4. 1 Peter 2:9–10, *The Message*
5. Psalm 139:16–18, NLT

Chapter Seven

1. Job 5:17, NCV
2. Proverbs 29:15, GNB
3. Proverbs 5:22–23, NLT
4. Philippians 2:14–16, NIV
5. Proverbs 13:24; 19:18; 22:15; 23:13–14; 29:17, NIV
6. See Hebrews 12.
7. Hebrews 12:10–11, NLT
8. Galatians 6:7–8, NLT

9. Proverbs 1:20–23, NIV

10. Hebrews 12:12, NIV

11. See Hosea 8:14.

12. Jim Bakker, *I Was Wrong* (Nashville: Thomas Nelson, Inc., 1996).

13. Isaiah 42:19–20, NIV

14. Luke 15:18, NIV

Chapter Eight

1. 1 Timothy 1:16, NCV

2. John 1:14,18, NLT

3. Hebrews 1:3, NASB

4. John 14:16–17,25–26, NLT

Chapter Nine

1. Psalm 84:11–12, NLT

2. Psalm 27:10, NLT

3. See Joshua 1:8, NASB

4. 1 Timothy 6:17, NASB

5. Matthew 6:31–34, NLT

6. Psalm 84:11–12, NLT

7. Ecclesiastes 5:19, NLT

8. Philippians 4:19, NLT

9. Acts 9:36, NLT

10. For seminar information, contact Strategic Christian Services, Dennis Peacocke, 1221 Farmer's Lane, Suite B, Santa Rosa, California 95405. Or call (707) 578-7700.

11. Philippians 3:19, NLT

12. 1 Peter 1:8, NIV

13. 2 Peter 1:3, NIV

14. See John 10:10.

15. 1 Timothy 6:18–19, NLT, emphasis mine

16. Luke 6:38, NIV

Chapter Ten

1. 1 John 3:1, NIV
2. 2 Peter 1:9, NLT
3. Deuteronomy 8:11–14, NLT
4. Note what the Lord Jesus said to the church at Laodicea in Revelation 3:15–19.
5. I tell this story in detail in my autobiographical book, *Thank God I'm Free* (Nashville: Thomas Nelson, Inc., 1988).
6. 2 Corinthians 11:3, NLT
7. Gordon Dalbey, *Fight Like a Man* (Wheaton: Tyndale House Publishers, 1995).
8. Ephesians 3:17–19, NLT
9. 1 Peter 1:3–4, *God's Word*
10. Ephesians 1:4–5, NLT
11. See Ezekiel 18:23,32; 2 Timothy 2:4.
12. See John 3:16.
13. John 15:16, NLT
14. Hebrews 2:11, NCV
15. Romans 8:17, *God's Word*
16. Ephesians 2:20–22, *The Message*
17. John 15:14–15, NLT
18. Isaiah 43:11,12, NLT
19. Romans 8:28–29, NCV, emphasis mine

Chapter Eleven

1. Genesis 50:20–21, NLT
2. Psalm 139:17, TLB
3. John 16:33, NIV
4. Romans 8:28, NIV
5. See Romans 8:19–22.
6. Genesis 50:20, NASB
7. 2 Corinthians 9:8, NIV, emphasis mine.

8. Acts 6:10, NIV

9. Acts 7:60, NIV

10. Acts 8:2, NIV

11. Romans 12:2, NIV

Chapter Twelve

1. Hosea 14:3, NIV

2. See Matthew 25:31–45.

3. Genesis 50:20, NIV

4. Robert H. Bork, *Slouching Toward Gomorrah: Modern Liberalism & American Decline* (New York: HarperCollins Publishers, 1996).

5. 1 Peter 3:15, NIV

6. Acts 1:8, NASB

7. John 6:44, NCV

8. John 12:32, NCV

9. John 16:8–11, NCV

10. Hebrews 4:12, NCV

11. John 7:38, NASB

12. Acts 20:35, NIV